ELIZABETH BARRETT BROWNING

By VIRGINIA L. RADLEY

Nazareth College of Rochester

TWAYNE PUBLISHERS

A DIVISION OF G. K. HALL & CO., BOSTON

To my mother, Lula Ferris Radley

CONTENTS

PREFACE

THE name of Elizabeth Barrett Browning brings before modern readers not her poetry, her prefaces, or her critical commentary but the circumstances of her life and her devotion to Robert Browning. Most assuredly she is cherished by generations of Romanticists who see her as one of a pair of lovers ranking with Eloise and Abelard or Dante and Beatrice. There is nothing wrong with this image except that it does not do justice to the artistic and intellectual qualities of Elizabeth Barrett Browning. In her own day she was mentioned in the *Athenaeum* as a candidate for the laureateship left vacant by the death of William Wordsworth; furthermore, letters addressed to Miss Barrett, Poetess, London, had no trouble reaching her; some of her poetry shocked Victorian mothers, while other works served to help bring about much-needed social reform. Far from being overlooked by her contemporaries, her work was admired by such Olympian figures as Thomas Carlyle, William Wordsworth, Alfred, Lord Tennyson, and Robert Browning, and by such subluminaries as Dante Gabriel Rossetti, Algernon Swinburne, John Ruskin, and Leigh Hunt. And there were good and sufficient reasons why this was so.

The purpose of this present study is not only to point out some of those reasons but also to introduce the general reader to Elizabeth Barrett Browning's poetry and prose. Because so few readers today are familiar with any of her works (with the possible exception of a few of the *Sonnets from the Portuguese*), time and space have been devoted to summarizing the poetry itself before attempting to explicate or interpret. The study proceeds chronologically in the main, taking up the juvenilia and early poems; the *Poems* of 1844; the letters; the *Sonnets from the Portuguese*; and finally those poems with political or social implications, ones almost invariably written during the latter period of her life. While the temptation to dwell on biography, as so many have done, looms large, such material is confined chiefly to the opening chapter, except where biographical facts are pertinent to the literature under discussion.

Acknowledgment of thanks goes to a great many people. Not all can possibly be recognized here, but each is thanked in spirit nonetheless. To Miss Anne Edmonds, head librarian of Mount Holyoke College, and to Miss Marion Munzer, formerly reference librarian at Russell Sage College and currently head librarian of University College of the State University of New York at Albany, my thanks for their assistance in the initial stages of this study. To Miss Hannah French, research librarian at Wellesley College, my gratitude for making materials available to me from the fine collection at that institution. To Dr. Lewis A. Froman, Former President of Russell Sage College, my gratitude for a summer grant which made it possible for me to see the places in England which are intimately associated with the activities of the young Elizabeth Barrett Browning. To my colleagues in the English Department at Russell Sage, my appreciation for their patience and fortitude when forced to listen to my monologue of minutiae concerning Elizabeth Barrett Browning. To Sister Helen Malone, President of Nazareth College of Rochester, my profound thanks for allowing me the summer of 1969 to complete the manuscript without interference from the duties imposed by the new administrative position I had assumed. And, most importantly, my thanks to Miss Vergene Leverenz for her unfailingly meticulous reading of the manuscript, her invariably wise suggestions regarding points of style and organization, without which my work on Elizabeth Barrett Browning would have been delayed for a number of years.

I am indebted, of course, to a great number of Barrett-Browning scholars, both past and present. I have acknowledged my debt in the notes, and I have attempted to annotate carefully each bibliographical reference. To John Murray Publishers I give thanks for permission to quote from the juvenile diary of Elizabeth Barrett-Barrett, and for permission to quote from the poetry of Elizabeth Barrett Browning.

VIRGINIA L. RADLEY

Nazareth College of Rochester

CHRONOLOGY

1806   Elizabeth Barrett Moulton-Barrett born March 6 at Coxhoe Hall, County Durham, to Edward Barrett Moulton-Barrett and the former Mary Graham Clarke.

1809   Moved to "Hope End" in Herefordshire with parents, brother Edward ("Bro"), and sisters Henrietta and Mary.

1810–   Eight more children born into the family of Barrett to bring the
1824   total to twelve; eleven survived to reach maturity at Wimpole Street.

1814   Elizabeth's initial efforts at poetry probably were exerted at ages four and six but surely by age eight.

1815   Elizabeth went to Paris with her parents for a visit.

1818   Kept juvenile diary of daily happenings and observations on her own character development.

1820   *The Battle of Marathon,* early poem privately printed by her father. Probably composed two years earlier when she was twelve. Seven of the original copies are extant.

1821–   First serious illness diagnosed as a "nervous disorder" by Dr.
1822   Coker, who prescribed opium; the drug induced a habit that remained with her throughout her life.

1822–   At work on *An Essay On Mind with Other Poems.*
1823

1825   First poem (other than private publication), "The Rose and Zephyr," appeared in the *Literary Gazette,* November 19. Corresponding with Hugh Stuart Boyd.

1826   *An Essay On Mind with Other Poems* published by James Duncan, London.

1827–   Father's fortunes declined; necessitated move from Hope End
1832   to Sidmouth, Devonshire, in August, 1832.

1828   Met H. S. Boyd, who influenced and guided Classical studies. Mother, Mary Graham Clarke, died in October.

1833   *Prometheus Bound . . . and Miscellaneous Poems* published.

1835 Autumn, Barretts left Sidmouth for London, to live until 1837 at Gloucester Place.

1836 Cultivated friendships with John Kenyon and Mary Russell Mitford.

1837 September, Barretts moved to Number 50 Wimpole Street, London.

1838 *The Seraphim and Other Poems.* In August, Elizabeth moved to Torquay for her health, with Bro as companion; Henrietta and George accompanied her from time to time. Uncle Samuel Barrett died in Jamaica; legacy made Elizabeth financially independent.

1839 January, a serious breakdown in health; given opium and brandy to quiet her nerves and induce sleep.

1840 July, brother Samuel Barrett died in Jamaica. Favorite brother, "Bro," drowned in Babbacombe Bay off Torquay, an incident which left Elizabeth prostrate; never fully recovered from it. Autumn, composed "Queen Annelida and False Arcite" for Richard Hengist Horne's edition, *The Poems of Geoffrey Chaucer Modernized.* Worked on a drama, *Psyche Apocalypte,* which she never completed. Also composed "The Cry of the Children" (published in 1842) and "De Profundis" (published after her death).

1841 September, left Torquay for London; rejoined family at Wimpole Street house.

1843 Several well-known poems appeared, such as "The Dead Pan."

1843– Collaborated with R. H. Horne on *A New Spirit of the Age.*
1844

1844 *Poems,* in two volumes, published by Edward Moxon; also American edition with a critical introduction by Edgar Allan Poe.

1845 January, received first letter from the poet Robert Browning; May, met him for the first time at Wimpole Street. Worked on *Sonnets from the Portuguese.*

1846 September 12, Robert Browning and Elizabeth Barrett married at Marylebone Church, London. Left a few days later for Paris; then went to Pisa in company with Mrs. Jameson and her daughter. Finally settled in Casa Guidi, Florence, Italy, their permanent home.

1847– Elizabeth's interest in Italian politics quickened; revered Cavour
1848 and Mazzini.

1849　Robert Wiedeman Barrett-Browning (Pen) born in March. Elizabeth met Margaret Fuller Ossoli and family.

1850　Mentioned in the *Athenaeum* as candidate for Poet Laureate. *Poems* in two volumes published by Chapman and Hall.

1850–　At work on *Casa Guidi Windows,* published in 1856; admired
1851　Louis Napoleon; interested in Spiritualism.

1850–　The Brownings traveled—Summers in England, trips to Paris,
1859　Bagni di Lucca, Venice, Siena, Rome—always returned to Florence.

1853　Worked steadily on *Aurora Leigh,* published in 1856.

1856　John Kenyon died; left the Brownings eleven hundred pounds as a legacy.

1857　Father died unreconciled with his daughter.

1860　*Poems Before Congress.* Death of Henrietta Barrett (Mrs. Surtees Cook).

1861　Health deteriorated throughout the year; died at Florence. Burial in the old Protestant Cemetery, Florence.

1862　"De Profundis" published in *Last Poems* by Chapman and Hall.

1913　"A True Dream" published in *The Enchantress and Other Poems;* available in *The Cornhill Magazine,* Vol. XXXVII (July, 1914).

CHAPTER 1

Biographical Sketch

I N THE year 1806 at Coxhoe Hall, County Durham, Elizabeth
Barrett Moulton-Barrett was born to Edward Barrett Moulton-
Barrett and the former Mary Graham Clarke. The eldest of twelve
children born of that union, Elizabeth was affectionately nicknamed
"Ba" by her favorite brother, "Bro," who was actually named for his
father. The first twenty years of Ba's life were spent at Hope End, the
family estate in the eastern part of Herefordshire, where she enjoyed
the luxuries and privileges belonging to her particular class. Here, with
her numerous brothers and sisters—Edward, Henrietta, Arabella,
Samuel, Charles, George, Henry, Alfred, Septimus, and Octavius (a
younger sister, Mary, died at age three)—she lived the life of a typically
large and robust upper-middle-class English family. To read of the
activities of the Barrett children in these early years at Hope Ends is to
share in a romantic childhood idyll.[1]

I *The Youthful Ba*

We are told that Ba wrote verses as early as four years of age, and
that at twelve she very likely composed her early epic, *The Battle of
Marathon,* which her father had privately printed in 1820. Of the
original fifty copies, supposedly only seven are extant.[2] In 1818, at
Hope End, she was writing her juvenile diary, "Memorandum Book
Containting *[sic]* the Day and night Thoughts of Elizabeth Barrett." [3]
This interesting document, now available in the rare book room of the
Wellesley College library, consists of about a thousand words; it ranges
in subjects discussed from the doctrine of innate ideas to the writer's
own character. To read the diary is to see that at the age of twelve she
had already developed the intensity that distinguished her mature style.
Candor mixed with an engaging humility permeates much of the
diary. It begins with a quotation from John Locke in which he discusses
the advantages of introspection and self-analysis. In reference to herself,

Ba states: "I have endeavored (I may say) to seek truth with an ardent eye–a sincere heart–of that I can boast, but I have never even in imagination looked into my own breast." She then expresses concern that such probing as she intends to do might result in excessive pride or in ill temper, but she does not permit herself to be dissuaded from the task: "I am not vain but I have some tincture of pride about me which I fear not to own, on the contrary which I like to boast of. I am not at all insensible to flattery when in proportionate degree but when outraged I am conscious of it–I prefer praise most when seasoned with censure as it then appears under the light of truth–I detest flattery when given by those whom I feel unworthy . . . I confess that I enjoy fame more than any worldly pleasure."

Undoubtedly, the young diarist did not expect anyone to read her journal for she continues to expound upon her faults with both vehemence and touching sincerity: "I am very passionate but impatience is my ruling passion. I can confess without shame and I am willing to repent and I can forgive without malice but impatience leads me into more faults than I can repent–but I *can* restrain myself tho' it must be with a strong effort–Perhaps I have passed over many very many of my faults, perhaps I have looked only at my best side. However this may be I know not but if it is considered that this is written with an earnest desire to improvement with an earnest desire of reaching truth, perhaps I *may* be forgiven."

In addition to the character analysis with which she provides us, we can smile at the glimpses into Victorian life she gives us. For example, she hates needlework and drawing. Dancing she considers "mere idleness." She states flatly: "I abhor Music," and she admits that sitting at the piano bores her: "I sit down discontented and I rise disgusted." We might well wonder what she did enjoy, and she gives us the answer. She adores Homer, calling him "more than human." And she likes Pope's translation of Homer, which very likely explains the verse form of her *Battle of Marathon.*[4]

For those of us who have drunk in the soft, green beauty of the Malvern Hills, it is pleasurable to think of the very young Elizabeth Barrett at Hope End, recording her thoughts in a diary, looking out over the incomparable Malvern horizon, and enjoying a vigorous and unblemished childhood. For, in 1815, Ba was apparently still a normally healthy little girl, capable of a journey to Paris with all its incumbent excitement. Six years later, however, the first of a long series of illnesses began; and, from this time forward, her life and happiness were marred by periodic ill health. According to Dr. Coker, her physician at that time, this early illness took the form of a "nervous disorder." He prescribed opium to quiet her, a remedy greatly favored by nineteenth-century medical men. Regrettably, she was to remain habituated throughout her lifetime, and this was to prove on more than one occasion more curse than panacea.[5]

From 1822 on, Elizabeth Barrett's interests tended more and more in the direction of the scholarly and literary. Like most English girls of her station in the nineteenth century, she had no formal education; but, unlike many, she sought to learn from her brother's tutor and from her incessant reading. In a letter to Miss Commeline, dated August 19, 1837, she writes retrospectively of her German sessions with Bro. She states that German is to be the "last of my languages, for I have begun absolutely to detest the sight of a dictionary or grammar, which I never liked except as a means, and love poetry with an intenser love, if that be possible than I ever did." [6] But, despite this strong statement regarding her antipathy to languages, she managed over the years to acquaint herself with Greek, Latin, Hebrew, French, and Italian, and in her later years with German and Spanish.[7] These acquisitions came about chiefly through her own efforts, but she was aided and assisted not only by Bro's tutors but by her great friend H. S. Boyd, the blind scholar who was so helpful to her in her early lifetime. Indeed, in a letter to Boyd dated March 3, 1845, she attributes her knowledge of Greek to him rather than to Bro's tutor.[8]

Elizabeth Barrett's renown as a Classicist was not to remain unchallenged, though her interest in Classical writings was never questioned. There were to be many critics in more recent times who would hold an opinion similar to that of Osbert Burdett, who, in *The Brownings,* registers appreciation for her enthusiasm for Classical studies, but none for her scholarship in this area. He maintains that she imbibed neither the spirit nor the form of Greek literature but that she treated it as a "romantic pasture" through which she wandered with great pleasure but little scholarly insight.[9] Although most critics of Elizabeth Barrett make this point, she would nonetheless be considered even by today's standards an exceptionally well-educated young woman.

Without question, she learned rapidly and effectively; for in 1822–23, at the age of sixteen, she was steadily at work on *An Essay on Mind,* a poem more notable for its display of erudition than for its originality or poetic grace. This long, quasi-philosophical work was not, however, destined to be her first publication. That distinction belongs to a short lyric, "The Rose and Zephyr," which appeared in the

November 19 issue of the *Literary Gazette* in 1825.[10] *An Essay on Mind,* like the *Battle of Marathon* before it, was probably partially subsidized by her proud father; and it was published in 1826.

Changes begin to occur at this time which mark the initial transition of the childlike Ba to the more mature, though still young, Miss Barrett. From her early twenties until she reached forty years of age, she was to live almost wholly within the family circle, leaving it from 1834 until 1846 chiefly in a vicarious way—through letters to her friends and through journeys in literature.

II *Miss Barrett*

In 1828, Elizabeth's mother, who had gone to Cheltenham Spa for her health, suddenly died.[11] At twenty-two, therefore, Elizabeth's status in the family altered dramatically. No longer Ba but now Miss Barrett, she became the mainstay of her father, a widower at forty-three. The affectionate bond between them, though formed at this time through mutual agreement, was to tighten into a stranglehold for the young woman. Nor was Elizabeth alone held in the octopean tentacles, for the rest of the family also suffered from the paternal grasp as the years progressed. Although Mr. Barrett appeared to be a typically Victorian *pater familias* in most respects, he differed radically in one: he could never bring himself to countenance the courtship or marriage of any one of his eleven living children. Nonetheless, for eighteen years Elizabeth took some comfort and found some strength from her father's obvious devotion to her and from his pride in and encouragement of her literary endeavors.

Originally, the family of Barrett had come from the West Indies, where they had exercised the rights and privileges of the landed colonial aristocracy whose great sugar plantations, worked by black slaves, provided them with wealth and prestige.[12] While at Hope End, Elizabeth's father, Edward Barrett Moulton-Barrett, lived the life of a wealthy absentee landowner; and all seemed serene and exemplary of the highest order of gracious living. In 1830—31, however, the family met with severe financial reverses resulting from the unrest generated among the slaves, particularly those residing in Jamaica at the family's Cinnamon Hill plantation. Although Mr. Barrett was never to become poor in any sense of the word, he did find it necessary to sell the Hope End estate and to seek and accept a position in London. This move, naturally, meant that the children also had to leave their idyllic sanctuary in Herefordshire. For the next six years Mr. Barrett's children were forced to move about; and their first stop was Sidmouth, Devonshire, in 1832, where they remained for some three years. The letters written by Elizabeth from Sidmouth abound in descriptions of a happy, close family who walk around the country and sport in the sea; and those years were good for Miss Barrett. In a letter to Mrs. Martin, one of her longtime friends, she notes that she is enjoying better health than she can remember for some time.[13]

The Barretts left Sidmouth for St. Marylebone, London, and finally settled in 1838 at the now famed No. 50 Wimpole Street, their permanent home. During these migratory years Elizabeth was busily working on poetry and making friends among the cultured men and women of her day. She was far from reclusive; rather, she was interested in and eager to embrace the current literary and intellectual life. In 1833 the earlier of her two translations of Aeschylus' *Prometheus* was published. In 1838 *The Seraphim* appeared, along with five or six short poems which had undoubtedly been written earlier, during the three years' stay at Sidmouth.[14] One earlier poem of significance, "A True Dream," was written apparently in 1833; but it was not published until after her death.[15] Two magazine items—"A Thought on Thoughts" and "The Poet's Vow"—were published in the *Athenaeum* and the *New Monthly Magazine,* respectively, in 1836.

The friends Elizabeth Barrett made during these years were, for the most part, enduring ones. Mrs. James Martin of the Martin banking family, who has already been noted as one of her chief correspondents, was known to her as early as 1828. John Kenyon, a man of letters of great cultural attributes, a distant relative, and a loyal friend, was her staunch supporter in years to come. Miss Mary Russell Mitford, English essayist and epistolarian, and Richard Hengist Horne, man of letters and sometime dramatist, were influential friends and lively correspondents. Of the above people, however, it was the genial Kenyon who introduced her to such literary giants as Wordsworth and Walter Savage Landor, and to the influential American scholar, George Ticknor. In a letter to Mrs. Martin (December 7, 1836) Elizabeth related her encounter with the first two men; and, in her astute comment on the meeting and on her reactions to it, she ascribed to Wordsworth "genius" and to Landor "eminent talent."[16] Somewhat later, she wrote again to Mrs. Martin of this rich experience: "I never walked in the skies before; and perhaps never shall again, when so many stars are out!"[17]

But these years were also fraught with illness and sadness, as well as with these fruitful associations and literary productivity. A dreary letter

to Mrs. Martin, dated January 1, 1836, on the subject of the Barretts'
move from Sidmouth to London portrays a depressed, forlorn Miss
Barrett who still had the fortitude to interject, with a somewhat droll
sense of humor, "I dare say I shall soon be able to see in my dungeon
and begin to be amused with the spiders." [18] Certainly, the summer of
1838 marked the beginning of her extended period of invalidism.
Although critics differ concerning its cause and severity, there seems to
be some reason to believe that an early childhood fall from her pony
had contributed to her constitutional weakness, but a burst blood vessel
in her lungs was apparently the most severely debilitating cause and the
one which mandated bed rest. [19] At any rate, she repaired for her
health to Torquay on the sea with her favorite brother, Bro, as her
companion, and her sister Henrietta and the "stalwart" brother,
George, joined them a little later. [20] From 1839 to 1840, Elizabeth's
health deteriorated rapidly. The attending physician, Dr. De Barry,
prescribed an elixir of brandy and opium and left instructions that she
was not to write at all. So she read. Plato, Aristotle, and Aristophanes
provided for her a rather mixed diet, scarcely one which modern
readers would consider light and relaxing; but to her they were "honey
dew." [21]

At this point troubles began to assail her in rapid order. For
example, in midsummer of 1838 news of the death of a favorite uncle
in Jamaica reached the Barretts. This uncle had left some money to
Elizabeth, which made her the only one of the children of Edward
Barrett Moulton-Barrett to be financially independent—a legacy that
was to have important consequences, as later events confirm. In 1840
her second brother, Samuel, also died in Jamaica. Then, on July 11,
1840, came the most crushing blow of her life, an incident of which she
could never bear to speak throughout her entire lifetime: the death of
Bro, whose small boat had capsized in the sea off Torquay, left
Elizabeth prostrate for months to come at that formerly idyllic place.
She blamed herself, for she had begged her father to permit Bro to
remain with her, and he had agreed. [22]

The extent of her suffering becomes sharply clear when, some
fourteen years later, she almost breaks with Miss Mitford, who in her
own memoirs had alluded to the effect of Bro's death upon his sister.
Concerning this reference, Elizabeth wrote to Mrs. Martin that she
could not bear such "obtuseness" as Miss Mitford had shown. [23]
Indeed, for six months thereafter her letters allude to her anguish over
Miss Mitford's indiscretion. [24] The literary result of the tragedy of 1840
was the poem "De Profundis," which sharply delineates Elizabeth

Barrett's sense of grief and devastation following her brother's death. Significantly, this poem was not published until after her own death.

In 1840, though besieged by misfortunes, she managed to contribute to a volume edited by her friend R. H. Horne, *The Poems of Geoffrey Chaucer Modernized.* Other contributors to this venture were Wordsworth, Leigh Hunt, Robert Bell, and, of course, Horne himself.[25] She was apparently also working at this same time on an unfinished drama, to have been entitled "Psyche Apocalypté."[26] Then in 1841, ill and dejected, she returned to London, accompanied by Flush, her much touted and beloved spaniel, a gift from Miss Mitford.[27] She remained in London, the captive of ill health, confined to her bedroom at the Wimpole Street address, for nearly five years. Whatever of the world she saw had of necessity to come to her, for she was far too ill to go into it.

The picture of Miss Barrett, reclining upon a bed of illness, is a familiar one to us all; but it is also in part a misleading one, for she did not lie idle. She worked on her poems, on a few essays from time to time, and on her engaging and astutely critical letters to her friends and contemporaries. The Frederic Kenyon edition of her letters written during this period contains reference after reference to her criticisms and commentaries, not only upon the works of her contemporaries (Wordsworth, Browning, Coleridge, Byron, Tennyson, Scott, Dickens), but also upon the works which she herself had produced and was producing.

That she had to conserve strength is made abundantly clear in a letter to Cornelius Matthews, the editor of *Graham's Magazine,* who had written to her in the hope of inducing her to write some critical papers suitable for publication in that journal. She rejects the suggestion, saying that she must confine her efforts to poetry in order to have strength sufficient to the task at hand: "That life is short and art long appears to us more true than usual when we lie all day long on a sofa and are as frightened of the east wind as if it were a tiger. Life is not only short, but uncertain, and art is not only long, but absorbing."[28] Despite this statement, Elizabeth did not confine herself solely to poetry, for in 1842 she sent *Translations of the Greek Christian Fathers* to the *Athenaeum.* At this time she also began to correspond with the American poet James Russell Lowell and with the English artist Benjamin Haydon.[29] Lowell eventually assisted her in gaining a reputation in America, for it was he who originally brought her work to the attention of Matthews.

One of her most successful and best known poems, "The Dead Pan," a work which took its impetus from John Kenyon's paraphrase of

Schiller's "The Gods of Greece," was composed in 1843. During this same year "The Cry of the Children," a poem of social protest, appeared in the August issue of *Blackwood's Magazine.* Other poems being written at this same time were "A Vision of Poets," "The Lost Bower," and the lines "To Flush, My Dog." Nor was prose neglected, for she undertook in collaboration with R. H. Horne to extend William Hazlitt's work on the great Romantics into a study of contemporary writers. Elizabeth Barrett was probably responsible, at least in part, for the portraits of Monckton Milnes, Wordsworth, Thomas Carlyle, Robert Browning, Leigh Hunt, and Harriet Martineau. The completed study, edited by Horne and entitled *A New Spirit of the Age,* was published in 1844; but it was not well received by the reading public.[30]

Elizabeth Barrett was by this time an established poet. The second week of August, 1844, saw the publication of a two-volume collection of her poems; and in October an American edition with a critical introduction by Edgar Allan Poe appeared. Almost from the moment that the poems of 1838 were published, she had turned her hand to writing the poetry which was to be incorporated into the 1844 volumes; and she wrote industriously, indeed ardently, despite her debilitating illnesses. The English edition of the 1844 poems was published by Moxon, and it established her as one of the consortium on Olympus. Furthermore, this edition prompted one of the most famous letters of all time; for on January 10, 1845, Robert Browning wrote to Miss Barrett to tell her of the deep impression her poetry had made upon him. His impetuous letter, quoted in part below, initiated the famous correspondence which culminated in one of the greatest love stories the world has ever known:

I love your verses with all my heart, dear Miss Barrett,—and this is no off-hand complimentary letter that I shall write,—whatever else, no prompt matter-of-course recognition of your genius, and there a graceful and natural end of the thing. Since that day last week when I first read your poems, I quite laugh to remember how I have been turning and turning again in my mind what I should be able to tell you of their effect upon me, for in the first flush of delight I thought I would this once get out of my habit of purely passive enjoyment, when I do really enjoy, and thoroughly justify my admiration—perhaps even, as a loyal fellow-craftsman should, try and find fault and do you some little good to be proud of hereafter!—but nothing comes of it all—so into me has gone, and part of me has it become, this great living poetry of yours, not a flower of which but took root and grew. . . . I can give reason for my faith in one and another excellence, the fresh strange music, the affluent language, the exquisite pathos and true new brave thought; but in this addressing myself to you—your own self, and for the first time, my feeling rises altogether. I do, as I say, love these books with all my heart—and I love you too.[31]

We can do little more than guess at the full impact of this first letter, but we know that it was considerable, as the following excerpt from Elizabeth's letter to Miss Mitford shows: "And I had a letter from Browning the poet last night, which threw me into ecstasies—, Browning, the author of 'Paracelsus,' and king of the mystics." [32] Moreover, Browning's first letter had expressed the hope that he would soon meet her; and her reply to him suggested a meeting in the spring. Almost daily letters ensued, and on May 20, 1845, the two poets met for the first time. Elizabeth's health improved immeasurably under the stimulus of almost daily letters from, and weekly meetings with, the handsome young poet.

On September 12, 1846, they were married: she, at the age of forty; he, thirty-four. Almost immediately the Brownings left for Italy, where her health would be given every chance by the climate to sustain itself in a relatively normal state. They took with them Flush, her dog; Wilson, her faithful maid; and her father's unrelenting animosity. Much has been made of his attitude toward his daughter's marriage, but he was equally unrelenting (as has been indicated earlier) in his attitude toward the marriage of the other children who dared defy him in this respect during his lifetime. Unquestionably, Edward Barrett Moulton-Barrett was a monomaniac on the subject of the marriage of his children; but, in all other matters, he did appear to be a typical father of that day.[33] His comment in later years to Kenyon regarding the marriage bears repeating: "I have no objection to the young man, but my daughter should have been thinking of another world." [34]

III *Mrs. Browning*

Throughout fifteen years of married life, the Brownings lived in Italy. Staying first in Pisa, they traveled to Rome, then to Florence, and ultimately made their home in Florence at the palace of Casa Guidi. That theirs was a marriage made in heaven becomes abundantly clear in the letters written to others after their marriage. Deep personal regard coupled with an equal quota of professional respect marks their correspondence. In 1847, in a letter to Mrs. Jameson, a mutual friend of both, Mrs. Browning writes that Robert has not been out during the evening in some fifteen months. She records that their days are devoted to music, writing, reading, and talking, and that she is far happier in her married life than she had ever dreamed possible. Robert, in a note appended to this letter, is typically the more prosaic of the two, as he ever seems to be in the letters; but he reflects his contentment also: "We are as happy as two owls in a hole, two toads in a tree stump." [35] After five years, Elizabeth is still writing of her happiness in marriage. To Mrs. Martin, in August, 1851, she calls Robert "husband, lover, nurse"; and she asserts that she has never had one single regret regarding her dramatic step. [36]

Their professional regard for each other is not less than these personal comments would indicate it might be. In a letter to Edward Moxon, Robert Browning wrote from Pisa on February 24, 1847, of his wife's writing: "I say nothing of my wife's poems and their sale. She is, there as in all else, as high above me as I would have her." [37] And she, in turn, was ever respectful of his work, believing (as none of us today would deny) that his was the larger talent, and that time would see justice done and his reputation firmly established. In a letter to Mrs. Jameson, on April 2, 1850, she comments on the "originality" and "power" manifest in one of her husband's works even though, she states, she is perfectly well aware that Mrs. Jameson may not like the poem. [38] Indeed, it infuriated Elizabeth Barrett Browning to know that Robert Browning was better known and appreciated in America than in England. In a letter to Sarianna, the poet's sister, Elizabeth relates the story of an Englishwoman who asked the American Minister in Rome if Robert Browning were an American poet! In this same letter, Elizabeth vents her annoyance and scorn that such should be his lot. [39]

Conclusive proof of their love and its benefits manifested itself in the birth of a son, Robert Wiedeman, on March 9, 1849, when Mrs. Browning was forty-three years old. Affectionately called Pennini, later "Pen," the boy absorbed many of her thoughts and much of her time in the years that remained to her. In July of this same year Mrs. Browning also bestowed upon her husband the poetic testimony of her love for him, a slim packet of sonnets, which they chose to entitle *Sonnets from the Portuguese*. Beautiful, though highly personal, they deserve the attention not only of those interested in the Brownings but also of those everywhere interested in lyric poetry.

The years 1849—50 found the Brownings traveling, first to Bagni di Lucca, then back to Florence, to Siena, and in November to Florence again. The year 1850 saw the publication in two volumes by Chapman and Hall of a new edition of Mrs. Browning's poetry; it was followed in 1853 by another two-volume edition; and a fourth edition in three volumes appeared in 1856. In May, 1851, another poem, this one with political implications, appeared: *Casa Guidi Windows,* which was published also by Chapman and Hall.

Travel to Venice, Padua, Milan, Lucerne, Paris, and finally arrival in London characterized the year 1851. Summer in London, winter in Paris, and then London again in the summer of 1852 were the events of the next year; but the Brownings never dared to risk the rigors of an English winter. For this reason, October, 1852, found them once again in Paris; and, during the winter months, they once again sought sanctuary in the milder climate of Florence at Casa Guidi.

In July, 1855, the Brownings once again set out for London to spend the summer, returning to Paris for the winter. In June 1856, they went again for the summer visit, and then home to Florence for the winter. This visit marked Elizabeth Barrett Browning's last journey to England. Her health, always precarious, became increasingly so in her final years, and it began in this year to decline rapidly. Nevertheless, her productivity was undiminished. November, 1856, saw the publication of *Aurora Leigh,* to which her literary efforts in the most recent years had been almost exclusively devoted. It is sufficient to note at this stage that the work met with an ambivalent reaction from the public; both acclaim and disapproval characterized its reception. There is no doubt, however, that it was considered one of the most avant-garde publications of its day because of its treatment of two controversial subjects: the emancipated woman artist and the unwed mother.

The year 1857 dealt a severe blow to Mrs. Browning. News of the death of her father came, and with it the knowledge that he had remained unreconciled to her marriage to the end. Until 1861 she continued to follow the travel pattern which the state of her health dictated: winters in Paris, Le Havre, or Rome, summers in Florence or Siena. Her final years were characterized by an almost fanatical love for Italy, one reflected in her fervent desire to see that unsettled country unified. This devotion to the ideal of unification was aptly expressed in the last work to be published during her lifetime, "Poems before Congress," which appeared in March, 1860.[40] While England had become for her over the years a place of sorrow and depression, Italy became increasingly a place of enlightenment, beauty, and strength. In England, she had been constantly reminded not only of her father's unrelenting attitude toward her and her marriage but also of her body's lack of harmony with the chill climate.[41] Perhaps her attitude is similar to that of her son, Pennini, who himself loved Italy always more than England and in his adult years made his home there. As a mere child he is reputed to have said, "In Italy, pussy tats don't never *scwatch*, mama!" [42]

Certainly, Italy was relief and release for Elizabeth. There she met and came to know such luminaries as Frederick Tennyson (the poet's brother), Miss Isa Blagden (long after Elizabeth's death a loyal friend to Robert Browning), Hiram Powers and W. W. Story (the American sculptors), and Margaret Fuller Ossoli and her family. From time to time she also encountered the Carlyles, Hawthornes, and Thackerays, as well as Sir Frederick Leighton, who later had the distinction of designing her sarcophagus. Many others passed through the portals of Casa Guidi, ever anxious to talk with its celebrated residents.

For fifteen years, life was rich and full for the Brownings. Intellectually, Elizabeth found interests she would never have enjoyed had she remained in London at the Wimpole Street address. By far her most consuming concerns were Italian politics and the far more suspect area of Spiritualism. One day, however, when Mrs. Browning's old bronchial trouble reasserted itself with a vengeance, she had no reserve strength with which to combat it. She grew unbelievably weak, then weaker still, until on June 29, 1861, she died in her husband's arms at Casa Guidi, Florence. In an anguished letter, Robert Browning wrote of his wife's death to Sarianna Browning on June 30, 1861. Strangely controlled in its account, but poignant almost beyond description, this letter cites her last word to him. It was indeed characteristic, not only of their love, but also of her quintessential self: "Beautiful." [43]

There is no question but what Elizabeth Barrett Browning was intelligent, sensitive, strong willed, and possessed of indefatigable courage. None who know anything at all of her would dispute this judgment. Attention is still being directed to her, both as a person in her own right and as the wife of Robert Browning. Her writings, however, are quite another matter; for poems well known in her day are now virtually unknown. A few of the *Sonnets from the Portuguese* appear from time to time in anthologies; intellectual and cultural histories occasionally refer to *Aurora Leigh* and "The Cry of the Children"; and some years ago in Washington, D.C., a paper was read at the meetings of the Modern Language Association in which sections of her poem "The Dead Pan" were quoted and received with laughter from the audience. While this study has no intention of eulogizing either the person of Elizabeth Barrett Browning or the quality of her poetry, it is hoped that a reassessment of her work will result in a more accurate appraisal of her literary reputation.

No poet's juvenilia is very exciting, and Elizabeth Barrett's is no exception to this general statement. Yet, she is a writer who did develop, and this development can be readily and steadily traced from the juvenilia to her first real contribution, "The Seraphim," as the following chapter bears witness.

CHAPTER 2

Juvenilia: Embryonic Poet

T HE earliest work of Elizabeth Barrett-Barrett is often derivative, as might be expected; but it is also often experimental. We know that she wrote verses at four and six years of age.[1] Very likely these early efforts were little different from the doggerel verse of any precocious young child who writes for her own amusement; for one of these verses her doting father gave her a shilling note.[2] Her first work worthy of mention, however, was *The Battle of Marathon*, an "epic" in four books, which was written in 1817 or 1818 when she was not more than twelve. She referred to it later as "Pope's Homer done over again, or rather undone." [3] It was dedicated in "gratitude" to her father.

I   The Battle of Marathon

The preface to the poem is a model of Ciceronian prose. In it, Elizabeth offers a brief statement in defense of poetry, the rationale of which rests in the belief that poetry is the sole quality in man which distinguishes him from beasts: "Poetry elevates the mind to Heaven, kindles within it unwanted fires, and bids it throb with feelings exalting to its nature." [4] The prose style of the preface, while labored and pompous, reflects an erudition astonishing in an author so young. There is little question but what Elizabeth was learned far beyond most of her contemporaries. We find none of the other Barrett children, for example, writing in this fashion.

In this perface, we can see that Elizabeth was concerned very early in life with the status of the woman artist: "Now even the female may drive her Pegasus through the realms of Parnassus without being saluted with the most equivocal of all appelations, a learned lady; without being celebrated by her friends as a SAPPHO, or traduced by her enemies as a pedant" (I, 2). Having justified her own right to compose, the young author then pays tribute to her contemporaries, mentioning Moore, Byron, and Scott; but she always saves the greatest laurels for

Homer, Virgil, and the "ancients." Their direct descendant is Alexander Pope (I, 3—6). She goes on to describe the characteristics which a historical epic should have: imagination, invention, judgment, taste, and truth. She then discourses on the subject of her own epic.

In the respect which she accords to the "ancients" and to Pope, she shows herself to be at this stage a devotee of the neo-Classical school of the eighteenth century; but her justification of her subject shows her to be devoted to heart over head, as many Romantics were. She cites her choice of subject, for example, as in "every way formed to call forth the feelings of the heart, to awake the strongest passions in the soul" (I, 6). This accent upon heart continued to be characteristic of her poetry throughout her lifetime. Here it is seen in her admiration for the little city that defied its many enemies so that it might remain free.

While her guide in the writing of the *Battle of Marathon* is admittedly Homer, it is Homer transmuted through the neo-Classical tradition of Dryden and Pope; for there is certainly nothing of the Attic element in her couplets. She defends her choice of rhymed couplets, in lieu of the blank verse of Milton, by saying that Pope "awakened the lyre to music, and proved that rhyme could equal blank verse in simplicity and gracefulness, and vie with it in elegance of composition, and in sonorous melody" (I, 8).

The historical incident upon which the poem is based occurred in 490 B.C., when the Greeks defended themselves against the Persians on the plains of Marathon. The Greeks were led in their defense by Miltiades, the commander-in-chief of the Athenians. The Persian hordes attacked the Greeks and attempted to force their way through the mountain passes into Athens. After nine days of unsuccessful endeavor, the Persians withdrew from Marathon to their ships anchored in the harbor. On September 12, Miltiades took the offensive and advanced with the Athenians against the Persians, who were guarding their ships and who were slaughtered since they could neither advance nor retreat. This event marked the first turning point in the long struggle of the Athenians against the Persian invaders. From here on, the West and Hellenic culture dominated the East and Oriental culture.

In her early and continuing love for things Greek, the young Elizabeth found such material fit grist for her epic, and she attempted to include various of the epic conventions in order to complete the requirements for writing in this genre. Because few will read her poem in its original, a summary of it, with its attendant epic conventions, follows: Both the "blue-eyed goddess" and Venus stand as representatives of *deus ex machina,* a convention indigenous to the Classical epic.

Pallas Athena's spokesman, the hero-warrior Aristides, advocates that the Athenians resist the Persians. Venus Aphrodite, however, has held sway over the Greeks since the Trojan wars, when the Greeks waged war in order to rescue Helen; and her spokesman, Themistocles, attempts to dissuade the Greeks from taking a stand. A portentous sign from heaven, however, makes the Greeks turn for leadership to the man of wisdom, Aristides.

Miltiades opens the battle with a war cry, "We scorn Darius, and his threats defy" (1. 90). In the name of freedom, the Greeks rally to this cry and fall behind their leaders, "Each Greek resolved to triumph or to die" (1. 300). From here the poem swings along through some fourteen hundred lines; and, though the couplets are imitative of Pope's, they are not unskillfully so. That which is not neo-Classic in temper finds witness in the youthful poet's love of gore. We cannot, however, ascribe this characteristic to Romantic extremes since Elizabeth had a remarkable precedent in the *Iliad* for such overstatement.

We are reminded of the feats of Achilles and Diomedes in her lines which show Themistocles' bravery in battle:

> And great Themistocles in arms renowned,
> Stretched heaps of heroes on the groaning ground.
> First by hand fell Delos' self, divine,
> The last loved offspring of a noble line,
> Straight thro' his neck the reeking dart was driven,
> Prostrate he sinks, and vainly calls to heaven.
>
> (ll. 1237–42)

A long epic catalogue of the deaths of Persia's heroes follows in the same vein. The final lines concern the Greek hero Cynoegirus, who attempts to stop one fleeing Persian ship by grabbing its beam in his hand. The Persians cut off his arm; but, undaunted, he grabs the ship with his other hand. When the Persians lop it off also, the bleeding hero grabs the ship in his teeth! Whereupon, the hero's comrades rush onto the ship and slay its crew. The epic ends with the cries of the conquerors ringing out over the plains of Marathon.

The poem convinces us that Elizabeth knew the characteristics and conventions of the epic, that she knew her Pope well, and that she had a more than passing interest in history, particularly in that of the Hellenes; but it more than convinces us that she had a long way to go before she became a poet worthy of the name.

II   An Essay on Mind

Regrettably, her second major work, *An Essay on Mind,* also does little to convince us of her ability as a poet. We are, however, staggered by her erudition. This poem was published when she was twenty, and she remarked in later years to Robert Browning that the poem was "more printed than published." [5] We can assume that her father bore most of the cost of printing.

Once again she works with rhymed couplets, but they are more flexible and less metronomic. The poem is shorter than the *Battle of Marathon,* but it runs through two ponderous books and 1262 lines. Book I explores the nature and quality of the mind, the differential qualities of individual minds, and the relationship of mind to nature and to idea. Book II addresses itself mainly to metaphysics and epistemology. The range and the depth of allusions to both past and contemporary poets and scientists are impressive.

The poem opens with the statement that men have ever been interested in the constitution of the mind, that they have always recognized with praise its potentialities, and that they have conversely been aware of its limitations. To describe Mind in the abstract, Elizabeth uses the terms "thou thing of light," "ethereal essence," "subtle cause." She asks that this power instruct her pen so that she may delineate the more specific functions of the elusive entity (ll. 19–40). She then admonishes her readers to survey the myriad faces of nature and "view light meet shade, and shade dissolve in light!" (l. 42). As bright sunshine alternates with black storms, so the mind itself, like nature, reflects various forms. Outward scenes are designed for inward sense. With this comment, the poet returns to the "world of Mind" (l. 62). Where she comments at this point on the nature of genius, she finds it to be fundamentally the same in all men of genius but to differ in its outward manifestation:

> Thus in uncertain radiance, Genius glows,
> And fitful gleams on various mind bestows:
> While Mind, exulting in th' admitted day,
> On various themes, reflects its kindling ray.
> Unequal forms receive an equal light;
> And Klopstock wrote what Kepler could not write.
>   (ll. 83–92)

She holds that critics, though not necessarily men of genius, are nonetheless men of accomplishment and are often helpful to poets:

"Bards would write worse if critics wrote no more" (l. 112). In closing the section about genius, Elizabeth enumerates the elements of intellect: Invention, Judgment, Memory, Association (ll. 171–81). Upon these elements Mind creates Philosophy; and it in turn includes within its confines History, Science, and Metaphysics. She capitalizes each, for each is equally important to her.

Men go to the past, to history, for guidelines to the present and future: "Important trust! the awful scene, to scan,/ And teach mankind to moralize from man!" (ll. 256–57). Nor must the facts of history ever be shorn of their moral implications. As the following lines demonstrate, Elizabeth embraces both the neo-Classic and the Victorian tendency to didacticism:

> Let Gibbon's name be trac'd, in sorrow, here—
> Too great to spurn, too little to revere!
> Who follow'd Reason, yet forgot her laws,
> And found all causes, but the 'great first Cause':
> The paths of time, with guideless footsteps, trod;
> Blind to the light of nature and of God;
> Deaf to the voice, amid the past's dread hour,
> Which sounds His praise, and chronicles His pow'r!
>
> (ll. 268–75)

While the didactic tendency is both neo-Classic and Victorian, the moralistic attitude toward Gibbon is purely Victorian. No doubt, like most Victorians, Elizabeth found Gibbon's attitude toward the Christians intolerable. He saw them as Fanatics who well deserved the fate they received. While hers may be an essay on mind, it is in every sense an essay on the *Christian* mind. Her Reason is Milton's "ready image of Right Reason" rather than the dispassionate Reason disassociated from God of a Gibbon or a Voltaire. For her, Gibbon is brilliant but misguided. As Dante could not proceed through the Inferno solely on the arm of Virgil, or human reason, so Gibbon cannot reach greatness solely by reliance on man's reason; and Elizabeth never wavers from the Christian point of view. There is ever an orthodoxy about her which makes even Pan a symbol of Christ, as an examination of the total canon of her work shows.

On the other hand, Pope's support of the *via media*, the balance maintained between reason and passion, receives enthusiastic approval from her in the *Essay on Mind*. A long passage elaborates on the theme that Reason is an efficacious power:

> Seek out no faction—no peculiar school—
> But lean on Reason, as your safest rule.
> Let doubtful facts, with patient hand, be led,
> To take their place on this Procrustian bed!
> What, plainly, fits not, may be thrown aside,
> Without the censure of pedantic pride:
> For nature still, to just proportion, clings;
> And human reason judges natural things.
>   (ll. 306—13)

Passage after passage reflective of Pope's *Essay on Criticism* or his *Essay on Man* unfolds. As Pope's Man was "Placed on this isthmus of a middle state,/ A Being darkly wise, and rudely great," so Elizabeth's Man is similarly addressed:

> Man! Man! thou poor antithesis of power!
> Child of all time! yet creature of an hour!
> By turns, camelion of a thousand forms,
> The lord of empires, and the food of worms!
> The little conqueror of a petty space,
> The more than mighty, or the worse than base!
>   (ll. 376—81)

To her, as to Pope, Man is a thing yet would be a God. He is at one and the same time, as Pope stated, the "glory, jest, and riddle of the world." For those who know Pope's poem well, the parallels in her poem seem very close to paraphrases. Nor was Pope the only poet upon whose work she drew; for, after the apostrophe to Man, she frankly echoes another of her hero-poets, George Gordon, Lord Byron. In *Childe Harold* Byron had declaimed, as did the early pilgrims: "While stands the Coliseum, Rome shall stand;/ When falls the Coliseum, Rome shall fall;/ And when Rome falls—the World" (ll. 1295—97). While much less effective, Elizabeth's lines seem more than coincidentally a stylistic echo: "Where stands the Syracusan—while the roar/ Of men and engines, echoes through the shore?/ Where stands the Syracusan? haggard Fate,/ With ghastly smile, is sitting at the gate" (ll. 397—400).

The remainder of Book I is primarily concerned with a discussion of the parallelism of History and Science; the pride manifested by science she deems unjustified. In addition, she emphasizes the importance of the whole when compared with any one of its parts, and she states emphatically: "*Dwell not on parts!*. for parts contract the mind" (l. 535). While such words may echo Dr. Johnson's admonition "thou shalt not count the streaks of a tulip" in *Rasselas,* and Pope's similar emphasis on universals, the echo is only implicit. Far more explicit of her mentor, Pope, are the lines in which she urges the reader to probe deeply. Here she parrots Pope's lines from the *Essay on Criticism:* "A *little learning* is a dangerous thing;/ Drink deep, or taste not the Pierian spring." She writes: "For too much learning maketh no man mad!/ Too *little* dims the sight, and leads us o'er/ The twilight path, where fools have been before" (ll. 584–86).

As the above lines confirm, Book I advances no new concepts and no fresh turns of phrase; and Book II is equally imitative, though certainly more complex. Addressed to the subjects of metaphysics and epistemology, the abstruse nature of its material makes it almost impossible to follow. In the opening lines of the second book, Elizabeth supplants the precept of Pope, "First follow Nature," with "Mind returns to Mind"—Mind must now turn in upon itself and contemplate that which is unseen rather than that which is seen; that which is seen are the forms of nature per se. To Elizabeth, the chief function of Mind is to seek out causes rather than to view effects, to see, as it were, "the principle of action, not the act" (l. 616).

Next she discusses the relationship of thought and language. Here some contemporaneity emerges, for modern critics might well agree with her stand. She deems pure thought to be obscure and demands that thought find expression in appropriate language. She makes much of the simple fact that words are the necessary vehicle of communication among humans: "Yet spurn not words! 'tis needful to confess/ They give ideas, a body and a dress!" (ll. 643–44). Without words, ideas remain invisible; for all intents and purposes, they are lost and locked in the silent crypt of the individual mind. Just as man prefers "imperfect government to none," so mankind must needs prefer words as imperfect vehicles of thought to no vehicles at all. Only in "some holy place" beyond these mortal confines may spirit look on spirit and engage in "voiceless intercourse." Until such time, however, man must cope with words as manifesting, although imperfectly, the visible body of the inner spirit.

Following these thoughts, she displays the antimaterialistic bent of her own mind. Sensations stand for her as analogous to the firelit shadows in Plato's allegory of the Cave. While sensations or shadows themselves are not real, they still reflect imperfectly the true reality, which is, of course, idea or the ideal. She admits, like Pope before her, that "We cannot reason but from what we know" (l. 766); on the other hand, that which we know is only a part of the whole. The power of

Intellect must discern, retain, compare, and connect. By this power man may come to generalize the unknown from the known, the whole from the parts. As she states, in effect, particular sounds which rise in concord make a melody which can then be generalized; in like manner, Mind, reflecting upon given objects, may generalize the unseen from the seen.

This power of Mind can, as it did for Blake, make it possible to "see a world in a grain of sand." For Elizabeth, reason alone is insufficient (as it was for Blake) for truth-finding. Here she takes *reason* to mean the guide or precept as man has established it, an eighteenth-century concept of reason. But, just as Coleridge equated this concept of reason with understanding, so Elizabeth sees it similarly as a lesser power incapable of discovering ultimate truth. For her, truth can be ascertained only by the individual devoted to its quest: "Men! claim your charter! spurn th' unjust control/ And shake the bondage from the free-born soul!" (ll. 811–12). What she means is that man, the individual, may find the teachings of John Locke and Plato to be wrong and, finding them wrong, need not err as they did.

In this respect, Elizabeth is a child of the Romantic movement. Her insistence upon individual self-reliance runs contrary to any preconceived idea of reason as the universal guide and ruler of man's soul. Man is to look to Truth itself to determine what is true, not to Reason as others have described the poet:

> But be not that dull slave, who only looks
> On Reason, 'through the spectacles of books!'
> Rather by Truth determine what is true,—
> And reasoning works through Reason's medium, view—
> (ll. 797–800)

After this discourse, Elizabeth turns her attention to the relative merits of poetry and philosophy. In her *Essay on Mind* she sees poetry as stronger and more effective than philosophy, for poetry relies upon heart, philosophy, upon reason. Not only is the value placed upon heart consistent with Elizabeth's line of thinking at this time (see p. 29), it is also consistent with the belief of the great Romantics. Coleridge in "The Eolian Harp," Wordsworth in "Tintern Abbey," Keats in "Lamia"—all hold the power of heart above that of head. More and more Elizabeth will conclude that the holiness of the heart's affections must not be violated; for, as she states, "the sage may coldly *think,* the bard must feel!" (l. 1090).

In addition to this emphasis upon heart, Elizabeth requires that poetry should look not only to nature for its inspiration but also to the relationships of men wherever these may be found: "To claim the interchange of thought with thought" (l. 987). And, finally, poetry must have its source within the individual mind of man, which to her is nature's glorious masterpiece—and again she is in the tradition of the great Romantics. Mind contemplating beauty finds that beauty mirrored in itself; therefore, nature imbued by the creativity of the mind, rather than nature *qua* nature, provides the materials of poetry. Here she might be said to emulate the approach of Wordsworth when he grasps the beauty in nature as both created and perceived by man ("Tintern Abbey" [ll. 106]). Thus beauty, for her as for Wordsworth is both within the mind of man and, at the same time, without; that is, it is seen in external forms also. For her, as for Coleridge, and later for Shelley, the shaping power of imagination is essential to the realization of beauty. She confirms this point in these lines:

> All poetry is beauty, but exprest
> In inward essence, not in outward vest.
> Hence lovely scenes, reflective poets find,
> Awake their lovelier images in Mind.
>   (ll. 992–95)

> Such poetry is formed by Mind, and not
> By scenic grace of one peculiar spot.
>   (ll. 1020–21)

But shining words and glittering techniques alone do not make a poem. A poem, she believes, must evolve from worthy thought. Translated into modern idiom, Elizabeth's statement might be construed as a forerunner of the theory that form should emerge from content. Actually, however, she is here the solid Victorian, believing that the prima facie condition for good poetry is noble thinking.

An Essay on Mind deserves little comment as poetry, except to say that the form, like much of the content, is derivative from and imitative of the Augustans. The fact that such a young woman would have read so widely and been able to assimilate so much material is, however, worthy of mention. We can turn, therefore, with few apologies from the juvenilia to the early poems of Elizabeth Barrett, poems which show the development of her diverse interests and which anticipate some of the innovations so typical of her later work.

CHAPTER 3

Early Poems: Climbing Parnassus

A^S WE move from the juvenilia to the poems of Elizabeth Barrett's young adulthood, we see the emergence of a poet of increasing critical acumen and verve. Those themes which engaged her developing talents were diverse and rich; and they accented religion and the religious, heroes and hero worship, as well as art and the artist. Sprinkled liberally among the poems of this period are touches of the occult, the demonic, and the Gothic. In spite of charges that she sought to emulate the "Sorrows of Diogenes Teufelsdröckh," [1] Miss Barrett was joyfully experimenting with form and content. Consequently, these poems show an astonishing, though chaotic, range. An examination of some of them chronologically and thematically reflects the turbulent and expanding creativity which possessed her at this time.

I The Seraphim

Most of her poetry belonging to this period is so little known that it is essential to supply the reader with individual, though brief, summaries before any critical commentary can be useful. Perhaps her most significant contribution, "The Seraphim," occurred as a result of her disappointing attempt to translate Aeschylus' *Prometheus Bound,* a work that appeared anonymously in 1833. In her preface to "The Seraphim" [2] she records the genesis of the poem, stating that, at the time she was working on *Prometheus,* she found herself thinking that, had Aeschylus lived after the Crucifixion and the Incarnation, he would likely have turned from the Titanic theme "I can revenge" to the Christian theme "I can forgive" (I, 164–65); for, as she points out, we know love only because "He [Christ] lay down His life for us" (I, 165). Aware that Aeschylus reflects "one of the very noblest of human imaginations," she still believed that, had he had a chance to understand the Christian context of "human-ness," or *humanitas,* he would have attained even greater heights than those he reached. As she contemplates the image of Aeschylus struck dumb by the infinite possibilities of the divine theme, she describes her own feelings of inadequacy for the task in her preface: "I have drawn no copy of the statue of this GREAT PAN,—[3] but have caught at its shadow,— shortened in the dawn of my imperfect knowledge and distorted and broken by the unevenness of our earthly ground. I have written no work, but a suggestion" (I, 166). Right or wrong, her attempt to stretch toward and delineate this "shadow of a magnitude" is in itself indicative of her early tendency, one later fully realized, to embrace controversial and often esoteric themes.

"The Seraphim" provides strange fare for modern readers; it is, unquestionably, a poem too arcane for our taste. Examination illustrates some of the reasons for its ultimate failure, but it also shows that many of its limitations are ours as well. To read the poem today is to enter a cloister where none but those members of the religious community know the language. Still within our ken is the Fall of Man and the Fall of Satan—the general matter out of which Milton wove his great epic. However, few of us are conversant with the seraphim, who received emphasis in the Middle Ages as the highest order of angels in the framework of angelology, and probably no one among us would dream of viewing the Incarnation and the Crucifixion through their eyes. Yet this is the expressed intention of Elizabeth Barrett: "Are we not too apt to measure the depth of the Saviour's humiliation from the common estate of man, instead of from His own peculiar and primaeval one?" (I, 167).

Taking as her point of departure Isaiah 6:2, which describes the Lord sitting high upon His throne flanked by the seraphim, Elizabeth Barrett weaves a heavenly tapestry in which two seraphim are named: Ador the Strong and Zerah the Bright One, who possess, as we might expect, superior sensitivity and intelligence. What they lack, "human-ness," she cannot grant them. Their lack of this quality, however, makes it difficult for us as "earth-creatures" to empathize with them. In this respect (and she knew this reaction might well occur), the poem fails to touch us.

Once the proper celestial atmosphere is established, however, we can follow the poem. It opens at the time of the Crucifixion, when all the heavenly host except for the two seraphim, Ador and Zerah, have left Heaven for Earth in order to observe Christ's suffering from man's inhumanity. Much conversation occurs between Zerah and Ador while the two attempt to understand why they are suddenly bereft of heavenly company. We are told that Ador has been struck dumb by the events while Zerah has been stricken by fear. For these reasons both have remained in Heaven, looking down upon Earth, which now appears to them as a place "God-created and God-cursed," a place of power-mad men and death. This literal Golgotha had previously been beheld by Zerah as a heavenly paradise, for he had been privileged to see it in the early days of Creation when it was populated by innocent Adam and Eve. In addition, he had been one of the Heavenly Choir who had sung at the birth of Christ. For these reasons he was named "the Bright One," even though he now lies prostrate in fear and trembling as he compares that earlier Earth-sanctified with the new visible Earth-violated. Here her characterization of Zerah rings true as she carefully delineates his essential makeup.

For Ador, too, she seeks to mold a definite character, strong and inviolable. It is he who attempts to wipe out Zerah's fear of Earth, and it is he who mentions the "tree without a root," that is, the Cross, and who reveals that the "crowned Son . . . walks earth in Adam's clay" (1. 231). Through Ador's words, Elizabeth Barrett meets her greatest challenge: she attempts to handle dialogue which tries to embrace the concept of the human, yet divine, sacrifice in order to convey the perfect integration of Man and God in Christ. The first part of the poem ends with the seraphim's achieving a vestige of understanding of this complex concept.

In the second part of the poem, the seraphim drop to Earth to view firsthand the scene of the Crucifixion. Complications arise for the reader when the supposedly wise and knowledgeable seraphim seem to have such difficulty grasping God's Divine Plan. Miss Barrett never fully explains why the seraphim have such trouble, but she clearly implies that they do not yet know that Christ is God Incarnate on Earth. In other respects, however, she rises to the needs of her material. For example, the fact that the seraphim in heavenly glory cannot cry human tears is a point well taken: they are, after all, sinless and lack "human-ness." They cry out in agony to God's creation: "Love him more, O man,/ Than sinless seraph can!" (ll. 695–96). For infinite ages the seraphim have lived in light and glory, unmarked by sin or suffering, as for a brief moment lived Adam and Eve before the Fall—such a situation would challenge any poet's power. If there exists a central tension in the poem, it rests within the esoteric question, "Can the seraphim know the agony of the Crucifixion as men may come to know it?" In a way, Miss Barrett grapples with the question of how many angels can dance on the head of a pin; but she does consider the question, as her attempt to conclude illustrates.

In the conclusion, she speculates about how angels react and feel. In the final lines, as Christ speaks from the Cross, saying "It is finished" (l. 957), Zerah states that the sound is that of victor rather than vanquished; and Ador notes that such victory is the Lord's. Here Miss Barrett concludes in a projection of what all humanity everywhere and in every age wish to believe, namely, that good will triumph over evil. The last word belongs to Miss Barrett when she demonstrates how fully aware she is of the impossibility of her subject matter:

> And I—ah! what am I
> To counterfeit, with faculty earth-darkened,
> Seraphic brows of light
> And seraph language never used nor hearkened?
> Ah me! what word that seraphs say, could come
> From mouth so used to sighs, so soon to lie
> Sighless, because then breathless, in the tomb?
>   (ll. 1020–26)

In an additional attempt to show that she realizes the magnitude of the task she has undertaken, she asks forgiveness of those very creatures, the seraphim, whom she has sought to characterize: "Forgive me, that mine earthly heart should dare/ Shape images of incarnate spirits" (ll. 1035–36). Alethea Hayter has commented upon the "strong, fierce imagination" at work in "The Seraphim." [4] Certainly, no one but Elizabeth Barrett Browning has ever had the idea of viewing the Crucifixion through seraphic eyes! While Miss Barrett may well have had an obsession, it was a magnificent one. Laudable for the images which transcend the mundane and commonplace, there are, in addition, loose pindarics which bespeak power and precision:

> And the earthquake and the thunder,
> Neither keeping either under,
> Roar and hurtle through the glooms—
> And a few pale stars are drifting
> Past the dark, to disappear. . . .
>   (ll. 995–99)

Such passages appear frequently in the poem, and these belie that the poem as a whole is a failure. The major defect in it arises from the selection of a topic which is, paradoxically, its strongest virtue. It took a mature Milton to plan and execute *Paradise Lost,* but Miss Barrett, thirty-two and relatively inexperienced, could not sustain the high plane her subject demands. As a result, the poem is marked by an overabundance of tears, by repetition of sentiment, and by a profusion of double epithets ("life-emotion," "Father-God," "calm-deep," "blood-bought"). While we do not expect the seraphim to speak like the man on the street, we are often irked by the far fetched, ludicrous dialogue: Ador to Zerah: "Beloved! dost thou see?– (l. 321); and Zerah's answer: "Thee,–thee" (l. 322).

Miss Barrett struggled mightily with her subject, and we feel her struggle in the frenetic overstatement so frequently manifest in the poem. Nevertheless, the poem remains a major one in her canon; for it marks her at this stage as one deeply interested in religious themes, in suffering as an efficacious power, and in spiritual love as superior (for the most part) to temporal love. This voice is, as Miss Hayter points out, her "authentic voice." [5]

A great many critics and biographers have commented upon the morbidity of Miss Barrett between the ages of thirty and forty. Irene Cooper Willis, in her brief biography of Elizabeth Barrett, attributes this mood to "the dreary gospel of suffering and sacrifice which she . . . propounded." [6] Miss Hayter notes that in the early poems "It would be hard to find a single poem . . . in which tears or weeping are not mentioned." [7] That the poet was morbid and that her poems are shot through with resultant tears is certainly true, and the question of why belongs chiefly to her biographers. Certainly she was ill for much of this period. The letters to Miss Mitford and to Mr. Boyd are full of descriptions of her precarious health. A letter to Miss Mitford in September, 1838, mentions that she has been spitting blood and that she is stunned by an "oppressive *sense* of weakness." [8] Another to the same friend in October, 1838, relates that she has been carried weak and fainting from the bed to the downstairs sofa by one of her brothers.[9] And in another, in 1839, she writes of an upset stomach which has made her feel as follows: "I felt oftener than once inclined to believe that the whole machine was giving way everywhere. But God has not willed it so." [10] And she is taking opium to alleviate this suffering. According to Miss Willis, Miss Barrett took forty drops a day during this period.[11] And in a letter written later in 1842 to Miss Mitford, Elizabeth exclaims jubilantly, "Vivat Opium!" [12]

Very likely this ill health did have its analogue in "weeping poetry," full of suffering and prayers to God. We do know that from the standpoint of formal religious affiliations Miss Barrett considered herself a "Congregational Christian." [13] What this means in terms of tenets held is that she believed in the divinity of Christ, that He was the son of God; she believed that the soul was immortal; and she believed that love was essential to man's reaching his highest state. She did not hold with priesthoods or with religious ceremonies; for, although she attended church in England when she was well enough to do so, she seldom, if ever, attended any services after leaving for her beloved Italy.[14]

II   "The Dream"

When we examine her poetry of 1836, however, we do not encounter discussion of formal doctrine; for Miss Barrett tends to combine Christian and pagan elements. One of the most interesting and best poems of this period, "The Dream," [15] has the poet speak in the first person: "I had a dream!—my spirit was unbound/ From the dark iron of its dungeon, clay,/ And rode the steeds of Time" (ll. 1—3). Here she travels backward in time through the great past glories of Greece, Italy, and Egypt. Beyond these, with their symbolic purport of beauty, fame, and power, she comes to the point where "earth was one fair Paradise." The earth, then washed in beauty, has on it birds and trees she cannot name; for they have passed from the contemporary sphere. All on that early earth is beautiful.

Later earth undergoes, however, a dramatic change; and, in her skillful handling of such dramatic alteration, we see in capsule why Elizabeth Barrett's poetry was so well received in her own time. The lines boil in metamorphosis and conclude: "Earth was no more, for in her merrymake/ She had forgot her God—Sin claimed his bride,/ And with his vampire breath sucked out her life's fair tide!" (ll. 34—36).

This strange poem concludes with the mention that sinful men have since walked on earth, disdaining heaven, and that only two or three among them have had the grace to rise above this miserable condition. At this point, Miss Barrett interjects one of her favorite myths: "For a God came to die, bringing down peace—/ 'Pan was not'; and the darkness that did wreath/ The earth, past from the soul—Life came by death!" (ll. 52—54). According to Elizabeth's editors, Charlotte Porter and Helen Clarke, she is alluding here to that myth first mentioned by Plutarch in De Oraculorum Defectu, where Ionian fishermen at the time of Christ's suffering and agony heard a cry ring out across the waters: "Great Pan is dead." Supposedly, after this incident the famous oracles of Greece were silent forever.[16] Again in 1844 she discusses this myth when she devotes an entire 273 lines to the subject in "The Dead Pan."

III *Poems on Heroes*

If we consider the death of Pan and the death of Christ as broadly encompassing the theme of the death of heroes or the efficacy of heroic qualities, we can read most of the 1836 poetry within this general classification. "Stanzas on the Death of Lord Byron," which reflects Miss Barrett's tremendous admiration for the Romantic poet,[17] sees him as synonymous with his own Romantic hero, Childe Harold: "He *was,* and *is* not! Graecia's trembling shore,/ Sighing through all her palmy groves, shall tell/ That Harold's pilgrimage at last is o'er—" (ll. 1–3). He is to her "Britannia's Poet!" and "Graecia's hero," who fought and died for the cause of freedom. Interestingly, the appeal to the young Miss Barrett is that of the youthful, esthetic, idealistic Byron; for we find no reflection in her poem of his cynicism, his satiric humor, or his sophistication. Nor did she leave Byron with but one tribute, for she wrote another poem in this same period in which she tells of the incident recorded in Emerson's *Journal* of one Captain Demetrious (an old Roumeliot) who, upon hearing of the death of Byron, burst into tears (ll. 1–44). Later, as we shall see, she does make some statements about Byron's worth as compared with that of other Romantics.[18]

There was certainly something about heroes and something about Greece which, when combined, caught Miss Barrett's interest. "Riga's Last Song" celebrates the death of the Greek patriot and poet of the mid-eighteenth century, who had wished to liberate Greece from the Turks.[19] He was betrayed by one of his own, but, before his assassination in prison, he defiantly claimed that his songs would inspire all Greeks to rebel.[20] Miss Barrett's poem has Riga viewing himself in his final hour, and his song of farewell to his country rings out in martial rhythm:

> I go to death—but I leave behind
> The stirrings of Freedom's mighty mind;
> Her voice shall rise from plain to sky,
> Her steps shall tread where my ashes lie!
> (ll. 13–16)

The names of Marathon and Thermopylae, which this section cites later, associate with tales of heroes and of glorious battle and death. And so Miss Barrett has written a swashbuckling poem somewhat in the manner of Byron's "Destruction of Sennacherib" or Whittier's "Barbara Frietchie." She has also returned to the couplets she favored so highly in her juvenile poetry. As a poem, "Riga's Last Song" cannot compare in quality with "The Dream"; but, because Miss Barrett later wrote so many poems about so many heroes, it is well to note it.

Turning next to Spain for her hero, she wrote "On a Picture of Riego's Widow." [21] Riego, one of the leaders of the Spanish revolution of 1820, was condemned to death for his participation in that rebellion. His young wife, a refugee in London, had asked the French government to intercede for her husband, but to no avail; and, after he was executed in 1823, she died, supposedly of grief, the following year.[22] Such a tale of pathos and tragedy appealed to Miss Barrett, just as the portrait (which she saw at an exhibition) enthralled Victorian viewers. The poem addresses itself to the constancy of the widow's love and to the hero's untimely and unnecessary death. Miss Barrett treats the theme capably in regular tetrameter quatrains. But, in 1833, when she turns to this subject again in "The Death-Bed of Teresa Del Riego," she writes a much more effective poem.

This latter poem is particularly interesting because of Miss Hayter's criticism of Elizabeth Barrett's heroines, whom she considers to be typically nineteenth-century women of fiction. Miss Hayter describes these women as blonde, long-haired, and weeping; they are noble, self-sacrificing, and full of ready blushes.[23] Miss Hayter is certainly justified up to a point, but not entirely. The widow of Riego is, for example, dark and pale; she is not histrionic, though she does weep; she does not sigh, she dies. Because she is the exception, not the rule, Miss Barrett found her a fit subject for a poem. The widow dies actually, not figuratively only. Many in the poetry of the day "die" of grief who are bereft of loved ones, but most die in the heart and not in the flesh. Miss Barrett realized this fact and knew that a romance such as the widow had known was not for the many but for the very few. Her lines: "Half to the dumb grave, half to the life-time woe,/ Making the heart of man, if manly, ring/ Like Dodonaean brass, still echoing" (ll. 42–45), hold the key phrase, "if manly," implying that only exceptional man can appreciate such love.[24]

IV *"The Vision of Fame"*

One other poem from the 1836 group deserves mention: "The Vision of Fame" a curious poem about fame's transience.[25] Fame, personified by a bright and beautiful lady, appears in the poet's vision and sings of the immortality which art brings to its creator. As she sings, however, her flesh turns old and drops away, leaving her only with a bleached skeleton; but still the vacant sockets gleam and still the song echoes forth. The poet hears, sees, and leaves the place in sorrow; but the poet cannot escape commitment to art, for she is irrevocably caught. Miss Barrett stresses in this poem the need for the artist to devote himself to his art, even though that devotion drains and depletes youth, health, and earthly joy. Here, too, we see early evidence of the baroque in her imagery, a characteristic which that appears from time to time.

The poems of these years announce themes that are to continue and to intensify in the ensuing poems: the death of heroes; the necessity for reliance on God and Christ for that which is truly worthwhile; the significance of love; the isolation of the artist. There will be other themes added to these, but these continue to receive emphasis.

V *"A True Dream"*

Of the other poems worthy of consideration, one is certainly that peculiar poem entitled "A True Dream," which was not published until 1913, when it first appeared in *The Enchantress and Other Poems*[26] after it had been purchased by T. J. Wise at the famous Sotheby auction of Browning materials in 1913. We can assume it was written in 1833 at Sidmouth, however, because the manuscript is so marked. This poem is not characteristic of her poems of the 1830's, and its singularity may be the reason Miss Barrett chose not to publish it.

Supposedly the poem is an account of a dream a poet had in which she practiced "magic art." By this practice, the poet-narrator has conjured from a vial a black-bearded man, of whom she is unafraid. Pouring a second time from the vial, the poet conjures a rosy-cheeked child whose kiss is hard and cold—a description that immediately recalls the succubus-incubus demons, whose touch leaves mortals with the feeling of having come in contact with hard, cold steel. To this demon in cherub clothes the female poet-narrator reacts violently, for she dashes the vial to the ground, and from its spilled contents three slimy serpents emerge and intertwine. Her brother, now introduced, points them out to her; and, bewildered by what she has wrought, she exclaims: "I have called up three existences/ I cannot quench again" (ll. 55–56).

She believes that this "unholy" company will stay to scathe her all her life. Her brother, however, offers to kill them with oil of vitriol, a burning substance. Although she prays he will not destroy them, for she knows intuitively their power, he burns them straightaway. They writhe and shriek as the oil sears them, but they "wax larger," and their combined wail resembles that of some soul in agony: "And glared their eyes, and their slimy scales/ Were roundly and redly bright,/ Most like the lidless sun, what time/ Thro' the mist he meets your sight" (ll. 75–78). In their evil agony they keep shrieking that they are stronger than she and that she should come with them. She prays and prays, in the hope of exorcising this evil; but their impious cries drown out her prayers. From amidst these creatures emerges a shadowy, dark form, and the speaker flies from him "with wings of wind." He pursues "with whirlwinds." She tries to lock herself from him in a chamber, but he breathes icily on her from the same side of the door! He speaks, "Who'e'er doth *taste,*/ Will *drink* the magic bowl;/ So her body may do my mission here/ Companioned by her soul" (ll. 113–16). With an iron weight on her heart, the poet hears the clock strike eight; and with that toll the poem ends.

"A True Dream" [27] is one of Miss Barrett's better efforts, but it contains, of course, some striking resemblances to Coleridge's "Rime of the Ancient Mariner." [28] The speaker acts when she conjures up evil; and, like the Mariner before her, she initiates this evil act. The child, ordinarily a figure of innocence, turns out to be a dreadful succubus who seeks to inject her with evil and to suck forth her soul. The first figure she conjures, the black-bearded man, does not approach her evilly; therefore, the speaker is unafraid of him. Evil, it is suggested, often comes disguised; the obvious is not always the true. Thus the child, though rosy cheeked, is evil; the man, though ominously black of beard, is not evil. The brother, despite the sister's prayers that he not do so, kills her creation, the three slimy serpents. Unwittingly, he adds to the evil already engendered. As a result, she loses both her body and her soul to the shadowy figure of evil incarnate who rises out of the burning snakes.

If any poem of Miss Barrett's reads like an opium-induced dream, this one does. But more importantly, it suggests that evil breeds evil and that evil is often unconsciously conceived and difficult to recognize. Regardless of such mitigating circumstances, evil gets hold of the soul and grapples it to damnation. Had the poem been written at Torquay rather than at Sidmouth, we might have suspected that it reflected her feeling of guilt for the death of her brother Edward; but the poem was written at Sidmouth in the midst of sunshine and during comparatively idyllic days with her brothers and sisters. For this reason, we must talk about the text of the poem and about its differences from those produced in the same period. Miss Barrett lets the poem remain suggestive of man's part in the creation and sustenance of evil in the world. While the imagery strikes us as strange by comparison with the rest of her poetry of this period, the sources for it are readily recognizable in the corpus of demonology and sorcery with which she was familiar. If any poem combats the characterization of Elizabeth as a bloodless, apathetic, young woman on a couch, "A True Dream" does.

VI *"The Poet's Vow"*

With something like relief, we read "The Poet's Vow," [29] which also appeared in the 1838 volume; for, in it, we leave the demonology of "A True Dream" and the esoterica of "The Seraphim" to return to an atmosphere more congenial to mortals. The theme of "The Poet's Vow," as Elizabeth states in her preface to it, is the idea "that the creature cannot be isolated from the creature" (I, 168)—a concept that is, of course, reminiscent of Tennyson's "Palace of Art" (1832). The two voices of Victorian poetry are the voice of the poet as moralist, seeking to take upon himself his share of world or societal responsibility, and the voice of the poet as esthete, seeking to espouse the doctrine of art for art's sake.[30] For Tennyson, his "Palace of Art" stood as antithetical to the voice heard in "The Lady of Shalott" (1832). For Elizabeth Barrett, somewhat the same antithesis can be seen in "The Poet's Vow" and "The Romaunt of Margret." The theme of the latter is also, as she states in her preface, "that the creature cannot be *sustained* by the creature." [31] Both of these poems first appeared separately in the October and July volumes of the *New Monthly Magazine,* but both were also published in the 1838 edition of her poems.[32]

In "The Poet's Vow," the central character, the poet, vows to renounce the world and all brotherly ties of affection. He wishes to atone for the sins of humanity and once more to sharpen and clarify that symbiotic relationship between man and nature that sin has clouded—indeed, demolished. He makes his vow in isolation, in a Gothic setting most suitable for his Byronic bent of mind:

> A poet sate that eventide
> Within his hall alone,
> As silent as its ancient lords
> In the coffined place of stone,
> When the bat hath shrunk from the praying monk,
> And the praying monk is gone.
>
> (ll. 19—24)

Like many of Miss Barrett's poems, "The Poet's Vow" is long. It moves through five parts varying from ten to twenty-two stanzas in length. Part II shows the poet emulating Christ's advice to the young man, for he gives to his friends all of his earthly possessions. But two among them love him truly and steadfastly: his beloved friend Sir Roland, and his betrothed, Rosalind. We are somewhat taken aback by the sanguine way in which Miss Barrett has the poet suggest to his friend and to his fiancée that they marry each other: "Friend, wed my fair bride for my sake,/ And let my lands ancestral make/ A dower for Rosalind" (ll. 138–40).

Rosalind's kinship with the human race becomes clear, however, as the dialogue progresses. Rosalind reminds the poet of what they have been to each other, and she also states her belief that "The teachings of heaven and earth/ Should keep us soft and low" (ll. 167–68). She sees the necessity for communion with earthly spirits in order to achieve that greater communion with God. As she stated in her preface to "The Seraphim," man knows love and God through Christ as man. But the poet, who remains steadfastly unaware of this concept, removes himself to a ruined hall, where he lives remote from human contact. There, in isolation, he watches,–Part III of the poem, the panorama of the world. First he sees three Christians pass by, and he ignores their call to prayer. Then he sees a bridal party, but he does not extend his blessing to the bridal pair. Finally, he sees a little child, symbolic perhaps of innocence and, more specifically, of the biblical text, "And a little child shall lead them." Here, too, he fails to extend his blessing. He remains studiously isolated.

Part IV returns to Rosalind, now bereft of her lover, who, stricken and ill, knows that death is imminent. After leaving instructions with her nurse to have her body conveyed, upon her death, to the poet's hall, she dies. In the final part of the poem, we see her instructions carried out. The poet, upon seeing the fair corpse before him, falls heavily to his knees. There he reads the scroll that Rosalind has prepared for him. In it she tells how she has prayed for him, for his love to move once more to a feeling for humankind. Finally, she admonishes him to show some feeling in order to receive God's blessing and thereby be with her in Paradise.

Reading this lament, the poet breaks. He rocks the senseless corpse "With the wail of his living mind" (l. 463). The result is twofold: a broken heart, and a broken vow. The poet dies of shock, brought on by his ultimate suffering and remorse. In the final lines, we see his friend, Sir Roland, bringing his small son to this double grave. There, when the boy prefers to look upward at the "wood-doves nodding from the tree," the father chastises him, saying, "Nay, boy, look down-ward, . . . / Upon this human dust asleep" (ll. 499–500). The intent of the father's directive supports the theme of the poem that only through participation in the world, through listening to the "still sad music of humanity" (although coupled with devotion to God) may a man be Christian in every sense of the word. To ignore the world is to enter into a sterile atmosphere that results in the death of man's humanity. This idea, then, is the message of the first voice.

VII   *Two Early Ballads*

In the companion, though antithetical, poem, "The Romaunt of Margret,"[33] Margret's failure lies in the fact that she refuses to recognize the transient quality of earthly love. She attempts to sustain herself by putting all of her faith in various of her fellow creatures. She will not listen to the spirit voice (which may well be the shadow of her better self) that tells her she will "go with light and life" if she can find one on all the earth who loves her as truly as does the sun, which is symbolic, of course, of that greater faith manifested by man but resting solely in God (see ll. 73–81). Margret rejects this concept and attempts to show that there are those who love her here on earth. She tells of the love of her brother, but the spirit voice that answers her every statement says her brother loves wine more than her. Again, when she does not listen but speaks of her sister's love for her, the spirit voice says that her sister loves her golden comb and her flowers more than she loves Margret. Still refusing to listen, Margret speaks of her father's love for her and is told that her father loves his ancient halls more than he loves her.

In this fashion, three of her fellow creatures are shown by the spirit voice to love material things more than they love Margret. Finally, she speaks of her lover, who is far away yet constant in his love for her. The spirit voice agrees but puts its agreement in the past tense; thus we know that the lover is dead:

> "He *loved* but only thee!
> *That* love is transient too.
> The wild hawk's bill doth dabble still
> I' the mouth that vowed thee true;
> Will he open his dull eyes
> When tears fall on his brow?
> Behold, the death-worm to his heart
> Is a nearer thing than *thou,*
>   Margret, Margret."
>   (ll. 209–17)

Margret's rejection by those lovers who belong to this world is too much for her to bear, and she drowns herself in despair. The ballad singer who has begun the lament concludes, in mournful tone, that human love fails, that false love too often walks the earth, and that love, when true on earth, is "deaf beneath the stone" because dead. The "Romaunt of Margret" haunts us with its melancholy tone. As a poem *qua* poem, it is more effective than many; for Elizabeth has wrought a poem in which thought and expression come together in perfect harmony. Here she is at her best. Miss Hayter points to it as a poem reflective of "the true sadness of the old ballads," and so it is.[34] Its eerie melancholy grips us in much the same way as does Tennyson's "Marianna in the Moated Grange."

Both "The Poet's Vow" and "The Romaunt of Margret" are much more effective than "The Seraphim." For one thing, they are less esoteric and therefore more comprehensible. For another, they are much more controlled and regular in form, and thus easier to read and grasp. "The Poet's Vow" proceeds in lines that regularly alternate iambic tetrameter with iambic trimeter. "The Romaunt of Margret" is more intricate, but it is substantially woven into some pattern of tetrameter-trimeter with the refrain "Margret, Margret" coming at the end of each stanza.

In her early poems Miss Barrett is much more conventional in her prosody than she will be in later ones. The early poems are not so imitative in form as the juvenilia, but they are, for the most part, regular. Later, we shall see radical departures in her versification. Double rhymes and erratic rhythm appear more than occasionally. It is not injudicious to say that she was one of the first to try new forms and to pave the way for that which has become synonymous with names now modern in fact.

Variations on the ballad stanza seem to have captivated Miss Barrett; the next few poems in the edition of 1838 reflect her preoccupation. "Isobel's Child"[35] again intertwines the orthodoxly religious with matter belonging to medieval romance, a mixture so characteristic of the early Elizabeth Barrett. We have seen in both "The Poet's Vow" and "The Romaunt of Margret" overtones of the religious as well as the accoutrements belonging to the romance—knights and ladies, ancient halls, and deserted manors. More often than not pale moonlight served as companion to pale faces and weeping hearts. The yew tree, favorite symbol of the Romantics, broods over Miss Barrett's rural landscapes and urges upon us her preoccupation with death and dying. The poet's Rosalind dies, the poet dies; Margret's lover dies, Margret dies; and, now, Isobel's child dies. Her use of the medieval is, however, quite superficial, as Miss Hayter points out.[36] The melancholic tone pervading these early poems seems to emulate the ennui which Tennyson's Lady of Shalott appears to be trying to cast off when she admits to being "half sick of shadows." For the most part, Elizabeth's melancholy is more that of a Romantic Victorian than of a Medieval scop.

"Isobel's Child" has no specific setting, but we may assume a certain removal of setting. It is not contemporary, for there are, for example, the castle clocks, the castle lakes, the nurse's pallet, the dark antechamber, a dark cathedral; there are hymns to the Virgin Mary; there are seraphim, cherubim, and fair ladies such as Isobel herself. And there is the mournful refrain which runs throughout the poem, with only slight variation, "Dully and wildly drives the rain:/ Against the lattices drives the rain" (ll. 233–34).

In brief, the poem opens upon a scene showing an ill child who has been surrendered by a faithful nurse to the safekeeping of the mother, who continues the night vigil beside the sleeping, feverish child. The mother prays that the child will be spared death, and the child does appear to improve throughout the night. But as the child gains in health, it also seems to grow older and maturely, though unnaturally, wise. The child speaks its new found wisdom and asks the mother to "loose" her prayer: "It bindeth me, it holdeth me/ in all this dark, upon this dull/ Low earth, by only weepers trod" (ll. 400–402). The child, having asked the mother to release it from her loving bondage, which God has granted out of pity, then tells of an apocalyptic vision of heaven and of the total sweetness and goodness to be found there. The final question which the child poses to the mother is in essence whether or not the delights of earth can compare in the slightest degree with the joys of heaven: "Can your poet make an Eden/ No winter will undo,/ And light a starry fire while heeding/ His hearth's is burning too?" (ll. 475–78).

The obvious conclusion comes with the peaceful death of the child. The reconciliation of the mother becomes manifest in the words of the narrator, spoken after the night has grown into dawn: "And a sense of tune,/ A satisfied love meanwhile/ Which nothing earthly could despoil,/ Sang on within her soul" (ll. 539–42). Both "Isobel's Child" and "The Romaunt of Margret" emphasize, therefore, the superlative virtues and beauties of heaven; "The Poet's Vow" indicates the need for human converse; and "The Seraphim" attempts to show the rarefied air of heaven while penetrating the very fabric of humanity. All these poems have in common one element: a belief in the fact of God that is one of the hallmarks of a devout Christian—which, indeed, Miss Barrett was. She believes in the efficacy of Christian love, in the necessity for suffering, and in the possibility of redemption. Her life stands, as do her early poems, on a model of Christian charity. In a letter to Boyd she states, emphasizing the importance of love in religion, that "the aspiration of Christians should simply be to *love more* rather than to *learn more.* . . . We shall be right in loving and safe in loving Christ—and happy in loving each other,—and glorified in love in Heaven." [37]

Over and over the modern reader is struck with the sense that the early poetry of Elizabeth Barrett belongs to another world. But it is not solely the world of the Victorians that has an option on her poetry. More accurately, it is the world of spiritual values which holds the cipher to her work. Miss Barrett was not so much interested in what the world was as in what the world ought to be. In this sense she shares with spiritual men and women of all time an apocalyptic vision. It is precisely this vision, as Miss Hayter has asserted, that makes many of Elizabeth's critics seek psychological reasons for her piety,[38] but there is no need to do so.

VIII   *Religious Motifs*

Throughout the 1830's, as has been indicated, Elizabeth Barrett devoted herself to writing such an incredible number of poems centering on religious themes and motifs that we could not possibly allude to them all. Few of them escape that didactic tendency characteristic of much of her religious writing, but in at least one poem she does try: "An Island." [39] She conceives of this island as a place of spectacular beauty, one where creatures may enjoy themselves in a fashion untouched by civilization and its attendant corruptions. A few kindred spirits who love poetry and art may share this island paradise, but only if they are willing to discard the trappings of a degenerate civilization and don the natural garments of Nature. Her tendency to moralize enters where she speaks of God as a superior teacher to Nature; and, in consequence, for the reader at least, the island paradise loses some of its attraction. The poem somewhat disappoints us, for we have been intrigued with the natural beauty of the island. We feel, in addition, that Miss Barrett almost gained access to a different world and then, at the last moment, returned to the comfort and ease of the known. From time to time, she marks herself, therefore, as a woman of her era, a Victorian, a Christian; but she does so without apology.

Far more successful than "An Island" is "Cowper's Grave," [40] which is distinguished by the solemnity of its elegiac tone and by the stateliness of its diction. For those critics who charge Elizabeth with a jangling ear for rhyme, the opening stanza provides strong contradiction:

It is a place where poets crowned may feel the heart's decaying;
It is a place where happy saints may weep amid their praying;
Yet let the grief and humbleness as low as silence languish:
Earth surely now may give her calm to whom she gave her anguish.

(ll. 1–4)

What arrests her attention and forms the matter of her poem is the thought of Cowper, blind and aging, suffering from the aftereffects of melancholia, and released ultimately through death to lie at peace in an English graveyard. While the poem is relatively long (fifty-six lines), she sustains the tone throughout and effects a kind of grandeur not often seen in her work.

IX *Lyrics on the Wing*

The refreshing lyric "The Sea Mew" surely is one of the loveliest of the 1838 collection. Sharply effective imagery surrounds the central image of the bird, enamored of the sea, its natural habitat. The subject of the poem is mournful: two people in a small boat capture and disable a sea mew so that they may transport it to land and watch its attempts to adapt itself to a different environment: "A grassy place where he might view/ The flowers that courtsey to the bees,/ The waving of the tall green trees,/ The falling of the silver dew" (ll. 22–25). But the gull cannot adapt and longs for the "Boundless glittering sea" (l. 34). Though the woman comes to show him love, he cannot live; for he finds human love "a strange, mournful thing" (l. 40). Some of the most satisfying images involve the gull in joy upon the ocean: "His heart upon the heart of ocean/ Lay learning all its mystic motion/ And throbbing to the throbbing sea" (ll. 8–10). Miss Hayter has remarked quite rightly in her study of the poet that Miss Barrett had tremendous empathic power. Of this poem, Miss Hayter says that "she could look at man through a bird's eyes. . . ." [42]

Another bird poem written in this same period is, however, less successful. "My Doves" [43] involves a pair of doves which have been taken from their natural habitat and placed in the city: "And now, within the city prison,/ In mist of chillness pent,/ With sudden upward look they listen/ For sound of past content" (ll. 31–34). Here, however, the doves respond to the human hand; they "almost seem to understand/ What human musing mean" (ll. 45–46). As Miss Barrett develops the poem, however, the doves become not birds but spirit-creatures, much in the manner of Shelley's "Skylark." In moving from the birds themselves to moralizing about her own immortal wings, she mars the poem with didacticism; and the lyric loses its effectiveness in the final lines. Later, she criticizes Shelley for moving from the human to the abstract.[44]

X *"The Deserted Garden"*

A similar, less than satisfying, conclusion marks "The Deserted Garden," [45] which Elizabeth begins by describing just that, a deserted garden. She speaks of the pleasure she found in it when but a child and of her unconcern then with larger questions. She tells of her favorable reaction to the beauty of the garden, a kind of animal pleasure and ebullience of spirit. Like an earlier spokesman for this sentiment, William Wordsworth, she also welcomes the sober climate which age and experience imposes on mankind. She states that "earthly pain" and "Heavenly promise" have acted as mitigating experiences for her; and, rather than deplore the passing of the garden with its simple pleasures, she welcomes (in an "Ode to Duty" fashion) the coming of wisdom.

Many have remarked about how unfortunate Miss Barrett's preaching instinct was. Yet, it was characteristic of the time in which she lived. If her preaching was too direct, it was at least totally sincere. And sincerity was a quality which she invariably reflected in her poetry. Humor, in general, must wait for the discussion of the poet as letter-writer; but sincerity can be spoken of whenever her poems are under discussion.

XI *"To Victoire"*

There is one little love lyric, "To Victoire, on Her Marriage," [46] which suggests that Elizabeth Barrett was no stranger to intensity even before the advent of Robert Browning. This lyric was apparently addressed to a friend whom she had met in France on that trip taken during her teens. Most biographers ignore this relationship; but, considering her age at the time, we cannot help but wonder at the lines: "I loved thee—for the Babel curse/ Was meant not for the heart:/ I parted from thee, in such way/ As those who love may part" (ll. 5–8). Whatever the meaning of these lines, it is clear that everything about this encounter was strange to Miss Barrett: a strange land, a strange tongue, a strange love, a strange moment. The latter is borne out by the words: "And now a change hath come to us,/ A sea doth rush between!/ I do not know if we can be/ Again as we have been" (ll. 9–12). But, of course, we know they cannot; Victoire is to be married, and maturity is with them both; adolescence has gone forever. What prompted Elizabeth Barrett to remember a love from so long ago, we cannot say. But it is clear from the context of this poem, as well as others addressed to the subject of love, that love was to her what it was to the hero of Tennyson's *Locksley Hall* and to Victorian Romantics everywhere: "Love is love forevermore!"

XII *"A Romance of the Ganges"*

For a Victorian "Romantic" to ignore the call of the Orient, of the bizarre and exotic, would have been unusual to say the least. And Miss Barrett was no exception. In 1838, at the request of Miss Mitford, she wrote a poem entitled "A Romance of the Ganges."[47] Written specifically for an illustration in *Finden's Tableaux,* she was supposed to describe a group of Hindoo maidens in the act of floating their lamps down the Ganges River in India. In the strange tale, she wrote of one of the six maidens, Luti, who had just launched her little cocoa boat (symbolizing eternal love) on the Ganges. The lights were to float softly until burning out of sight; for, if one failed to float, the lover of the maiden has been false to his loved one who is launching the light. When Luti's light goes out, she cries to the seventh maiden, Nuleeni, to right her boat and thus prove her lover true. It seems that Nuleeni's love, however, is also Luti's love, and that the lover who is false to Luti is true to Nuleeni, as the brightly burning lamp of the latter illustrates. From this sign Luti guesses the truth, for she has heard Nuleeni murmur the lover's name in her sleep. Luti, therefore, informs Nuleeni that a lover false to one is likely to be false to the next. For this reason, Nuleeni is bereft of joy in the final lines of the poem in which we are told that, though her light burns brightly, "She weepeth dark with sorrow" (l. 212).

Combined with this Romantic setting is a realistic treatment of human treachery in love. Elizabeth Barrett has taken a Romantic theme in a Romantic setting and injected it with the kind of realism that is so characteristic of her later poems of social protest. If we seek evidence of thematic development, we might look to "A Romance of the Ganges" as a harbinger. By the time the poems of 1838 were in circulation, Elizabeth Barrett had achieved a small measure of renown among family and friends. But it remained for the *Poems* of 1844 to appear before she began to be a poet recognized not only by those who loved her but also by the reading public at large. We have seen that her early poems, while they reflect a vast though chaotic range, are highly unselective with respect to theme, tone, and refinement. The discussion of her *Poems* of 1844, which follows, demonstrates increasing selectivity, sharper focus, and greater sensitivity and polish. In short, we witness the poet's climb, some six years later, slowly but steadily up Parnassus.

CHAPTER 4

A More Vigorous Voice: The Poems of 1844

WITH the publication of *Poems* in 1844, Elizabeth Barrett Barrett was established in the affections of English readers. In this year preceding her introduction to the man who would change her life, she published some of her most popular poems: "The Romaunt of the Page," "The Lay of the Brown Rosary," "The Rhyme of the Duchess May," "Lady Geraldine's Courtship," "The Cry of the Children," "Catarina to Camoëns," "Wine of Cyprus," and "The Dead Pan." Of most of these we have at least heard, although the comment, made by Virginia Woolf, that " 'Lady Geraldine's Courtship' is glanced at perhaps by two professors in American universities once a year," [1] is particularly damning when we note that it was made over thirty years ago. Nonetheless, several of these poems are worthy of consideration, and not solely for their historical interest. Miss Hayter remarks that it is "almost impossible now not to dislike these poems very much indeed." [2] But she discusses with fairness the attractions of the ballads among the group. She makes the point that Elizabeth herself did not like them, but that the strong, "narrative sweep" very likely endeared them to people who were not generally readers of poetry. [3]

Miss Hayter is unquestionably right about the attractions of narrative poetry in the nineteenth century. Most readers appreciated it. When we consider our own American household poets, we think of Longfellow, Lowell, Whittier, Holmes; and we know the enormous appeal that certain of their potboilers had for nineteenth-century Americans. When we turn to the same consideration of Elizabeth's countrymen, we recall that Tennyson's "Locksley Hall," Arnold's "Sohrab and Rustum," and others of their kind enjoyed a popularity far in excess of the reception that Stephen Vincent Benét's *John Brown's Body* enjoyed in our own time. Whatever the reasons, the twentieth-century reader (except in the nation's junior high schools) does not find narrative poetry exciting enough to read it; and this change in intellectual climate has wrought havoc with those poems of

Elizabeth Barrett's that enjoyed such favor in her own day. We can still, however, enjoy them if we know whereof they speak and, more simply, what they are about. To accomplish this end, we must consider the poetry before we attempt to criticize it.

I *"The Romaunt of the Page"*

"The Romaunt of the Page" [4] contains much action, and it begins when a young page rides off with a knight to Palestine. En route, the knight tells that he has married the daughter of his father's best friend and that his father was killed while avenging his friend's honor. The knight has not had the chance to know his wife, for he had left immediately after the wedding for Palestine. The page tells that his sister has followed her knight into battle, but the knight scornfully states that his "ladye" would never do such a thing, for he himself would not wish an "unwomaned" woman.

We are relatively sure by this time that the page is in fact the knight's wife in disguise—and so "he" is. The bride has come to accompany her knight as a testament of her true love for him. She realizes, however, that he will never accept what she has done for him because he appears to believe "That womanhood is proved the best/ By golden brooch and glossy vest/ The minding ladies wear" (ll. 199–201). And so, disconsolate, she watches him ride off. He hopes to escape a horde of Paynims who dash at them, while she remains behind on the pretext of adjusting her saddle. As she awaits death at these alien hands, she prays for her thoughtless lover.

> Yet God thee save, and mayst thou have
> A lady to thy mind,
> More woman-proud and half as true
> As one thou leav'st behind!
> (ll. 280–83)

We can easily see that people would be attracted to this poem for many of the same reasons that scores of readers have been attracted to Whittier's "Barbara Frietchie," Longfellow's "Excelsior," and the like. There is no startlingly fresh imagery, but there is a well-told tale that evinces a facility that makes the lines run along quickly and smoothly. [5]

II *"The Lay of the Brown Rosary"*

"The Lay of the Brown Rosary" [6] has more to recommend it than "The Romaunt of the Page." We are introduced in it to a young maiden, Onora, whose mother is calling for her; but she is told by her young son that Onora will not come because she is sitting with the "nun of the brown rosary." As the little boy speaks, he bursts into tears; for the nun is a symbol of evil, as is the setting, an old convent ruin, heavily Gothic and evil in implication. A nun has been buried in the wall long ago, but she rises like a vampire at night to cast her spell over Onora, who wills that her lover be bound to her. In this way Onora has, as two angels explain in Part II, bartered God's love for that of a man. She is tortured by what she has done; and, at night, not only the angels but also the spirit of the dead nun visit her. She dreams that her father, who lies buried in the courtyard, asks her to walk into the fields with him. The nun, hearing about this dream, cries: "Forbear that dream—forbear that dream!" But visions of a sweet and pure childhood in nature still flash before Onora's eyes, all images reminiscent of an earlier innocence. The veiled nun now makes her repeat the vow she has made, and she does: "I vowed to thee on rosary (dead father look not so!),/ I *would not thank God in my weal, nor seek God in my woe*" (ll. 206–7). Having spoken these words, she catches sight of her lover on his prancing steed.

We know, however, that she has sold her soul to the devil and that Part III must, for that reason, end in tragedy, even though it opens with wedding bells. We expect Onora to be exposed by innocence, and so she is. As she is about to wed her lover, her little brother rushes in to call her vile before the company, the priest, and the carved saints in the church niches. Asked to prove his charges, he refers to the brown rosary she wears. The priest remonstrates with him, saying that a brown rosary is more fitting than an ornate one. The ceremony begins, the priest reads from the psalter; but he cannot read the word "God"! The wedding guests note that Onora is standing silent, not repeating the prayers, and that she looks cold and remote. As the priest finishes, thinking he has sinned in some unknown way and hence is unable to say "God," the groom kisses the bride and falls dead. She, in a frenzy of grief and remorse, dashes the brown rosary to the marble floor. From here on, she declines in her home, under the sad eyes of her mother and brother, until she dies. We are told that she, like the flower she had placed on her lover's tomb, "perished mute for lack of root, earth's nourishment to reach" (l. 401).

Elizabeth's Barrett's knowledge of witchcraft and demonology is evident throughout "The Lay of the Brown Rosary." For example, the little brother's hound shies away from the ruined convent, an act indicative of the supposed supersensitivity to evil which animals have.

The dead nun leaves her grave in the wall when night comes, as vampires and demons are traditionally prone to do. The brown rosary itself seems imbued with evil properties. As in most works with demonic properties, the symbols are overly simplified. The young boy, Onora's brother, represents uncorrupted innocence; and the grey nun of the brown rosary is obviously evil incarnate. Onora herself becomes the agent of evil when she makes a pact with the devil nun by vowing to reject God in exchange for the love of man, her knight on his prancing steed. The ending is traditional in that Onora, through consorting with evil, brings tragedy to the ones she loves the most. This is a poem in the tradition of Keats's "Lamia," his "La Belle Dame sans Merci," Coleridge's "Christabel" and "Lewti," and countless others which invoke the "demon-lover." Miss Barrett herself recognized that this poem was "full of faults," [7] and she stated that the subject of "The Romaunt" was not of her "choosing," [8] for unquestionably, she looked upon both poems as potboilers; in a sense, they were. Popular with the people yet reviled by the critics, they still have merit for the entertainment they provide.

III   *"Lady Geraldine's Courtship"*

In a letter to John Kenyon of November 8, 1844, Elizabeth remarked of "Lady Geraldine's Courtship" that "the poem has had more attention than its due." [9] She had dashed off some one hundred and forty lines of the poem in a day in order to plump out the second volume of the 1844 *Poems.* [10] She knew, therefore, that the poem was hurriedly and perhaps sloppily composed. She defended it solely on the basis that it was modern, calling it " 'a romance of the age,' treating of railroads, routes, and all manner of 'temporalities,' and in so radical a temper that I expect to be reproved for it by the Conservative reviews round." [11] Far from being "reproved" by the people, however, she was astonished to find that "Lady Geraldine's Courtship" was the favorite not only of commoners but also of such luminaries as Thomas and Jane Carlyle and Harriet Martineau. [12] For us, however, the poem is interesting as a kind of precursor of Elizabeth's *Aurora Leigh.* There is no question but that she had in mind at this time the idea of writing a long, verse novel that would treat contemporary problems, no matter how controversial they might be or how much they might scandalize the reading public. In letters to Robert Browning [13] and to John Kenyon [14] she comments fully upon her intention to write such a work, and "Lady Geraldine's Courtship" seems to have been a kind of trial balloon.

Those who approach "Lady Geraldine's Courtship" [15] today find it lacking in substance, its characters flat and flimsy. From his room in Wycomb Hall, a young, love-sick, languishing poet writes to a friend of his love for the lady of the manor, Lady Geraldine. An earl's daughter, rich, proud, and noble, "she treads the crimson carpet and she breathes the perfumed air" (l. 6). He goes on in this letter to catalogue her virtues and, moreover, her vast holdings. We can readily see in the following stanza why John Kenyon protested to Elizabeth that he had difficulty following the poem; its long lines rollick and jog along, scarcely connoting the state of mind of the young peasant-poet:

> She has halls among the woodlands, she has castles by the breakers,
> She has farms and she has manors, she can threaten and command:
> And the palpitating engines snort in steam across her acres,
> As they mark upon the blasted heaven the measure of the land.
>
> (ll. 9–12)

Almost everyone has noted the change in the stanza from the earlier "and the resonant steam eagles/ Follow far on the directing of her floating dove-like hand," which might, had it been allowed to stand, have constituted the worst line in English poetry. [16]

We learn next that the peasant-poet, Mr. Bertram, has been invited to the hall by the regal Lady Geraldine. He is to sing his poetry, accompanied by the thrushes in the beautiful wood surrounding the castle. Like the hero of "Locksley Hall," the young poet often sits in isolation from the merry and well-endowed group of aristocrats in residence while he languishes in his love for Lady Geraldine. From time to time he reads not only from his own poetry, but also from that of Spenser, Petrarch, Wordsworth, Tennyson, and Browning, while the lady listens attentively in the wood or hall. An allusion to the last of these poets was the line that flattered Robert Browning, arrested his attention, and caused him to write the famous first letter to Elizabeth Barrett. The line reads "Or from Browning some 'Pomegranate,' which, if cut deep down the middle,/ Shows a heart within blood-tinctured, of a veined humanity" (II, ll. 161–64).

Bertram and Lady Geraldine talk about poetry, metaphysics, social conditions, and truth. However, the lady appears to have many suitors; and one among them, who pursues her vigorously, is "her kind," with aristocratic, cold, good looks. We see him through the eyes of the young poet and hear the conversation between this man and Lady Geraldine through the poet's ears. When the lady tells the lord that she will marry only a man who is noble and wealthy, the poet is stung to madness. In a dramatic, brutal tirade, he castigates her for what he supposes to be her materialistic nature. As he rises to a crescendo of rage, she speaks his name with tears in her eyes: "Bertram." Hearing it, he faints dead away at her feet, so surprised is he by her sweet compassion, so startled by her kindness. In his room, he finishes the letter at this point, and the Lady Geraldine appears to him in a vision. She speaks to him, saying that she loves him and that he is all that she has vowed she wants in a husband. The poem ends with an adoring Bertram, on the floor before her, listening to her low whisper of triumph: "It shall be as I have sworn./ Very rich he is in virtues, very noble—noble, certes;/ And I shall not blush in knowing that men call him lowly born" (II, 410–12).

In 1897 Frederic Kenyon referred to "Lady Geraldine's Courtship" as "that masterpiece of rhetorical sentimentality." [17] Almost seventy years later, we cannot find much more to say. Undoubtedly, the character of Bertram, so pallid, weak, and one-dimensional, is irritating. It is difficult, if not impossible, to see how the imperious Lady Geraldine, with her halls, castles, lands, and railroads, could possibly love such a puny character. We are more than willing to agree with Edmund Clarence Stedman's hilarious estimate that "Bertram is a dreadful prig, who cries, mouths, and faints like a school-girl, allowing himself to eat the bread of the Philistines and betray his sense of inequality, and upon whom Lady Geraldine certainly throws herself away. He is a libel upon the whole race of poets." [18]

On the other hand, it was high time that the reverse Cinderella theme came into being. While the poem scarcely strikes us as "daring," there is no question that the rigid class system received a considerable jolt from "Lady Geraldine's Courtship." Long before D. H. Lawrence's Mellors got Lady Chatterley to run off with him, Elizabeth was, so to speak, setting the stage for the action in a time when a lady did not run off with the coachman and receive favor from Victorian audiences. Today, this situation is laughable; but, to staid Victorians, such behavior belonged properly, if at all, in fairy tales. For all that can be said against the poem, Elizabeth is to be congratulated for her courage, if not for her poetic prowess.

IV   *"The Cry of the Children"*

Courage she had, and she displayed it in pursuing the diverse themes of the *Poems* of 1844. Most distressing to her, as to humanitarians everywhere, were the conditions under which children spun out their lives in factories and in mines under grueling and inhuman conditions. G. M. Young in his magnificent essay, *Portrait of an Age*, quite rightly assesses the kind of man who would keep children of nine working nine hours a day in 98-degree heat.[19] This common and accepted practice meant cheap labor and cheap production, which ultimately would benefit the poor everywhere. Thus the end justified the means, according to the British industrialists. It was, therefore, courageous for Elizabeth to write and publish "The Cry of the Children" in an effort to assist the passage of an act which would regulate the hours and conditions under which children could be put to work. She had never been in a mine or a factory; her information came from a report prepared by R. H. Horne about the employment of children and young persons in mines and "manufactories." This report, with the aid of her poem, very likely helped pass the long-needed legislation.[20]

In view of her limited experience with the working class and its attendant conditions, it is surprising that "The Cry of the Children"[21] so effectively catches and recapitulates the sorrows and harshness endured by the children. As she was well aware, the rhyme and rhythm of the poem "wants melody . . . [and] is eccentric to the ear."[22] These characteristics, however, need not be regarded as faults, for the subject itself is "miserable" and wretched, harsh, and grating. Throughout the poem she utilizes the wheel image, an industrial wheel which grinds the innocent children who work beneath it as inhumanly as it does its given materials. The children weep in hopeless acceptance of their lot. While all the young of nature—lambs, fawns, and birds—frolic in the sun, the young of man work in darkness and heat, their lives vitiated by their labor. In a particularly effective stanza, the children speak of the monotonous but laborious conditions under which they work:

> For all day the wheels are droning, turning;
>   Their wind comes in our faces,
> Till our hearts turn, our heads with pulses burning,
>   And the walls turn in their places:
> Turns the sky in the high window, blank and reeling,
>   Turns the long light that drops adown the wall,
> Turn the black flies that crawl along the ceiling:
>   All are turning, all the day, and we with all.
> And all day the iron wheels are droning,
>   And sometimes we could pray,
> "O ye wheels" (breaking out in a mad moaning),
>   "Stop! be silent for to-day!"
>   (ll. 77–88)

But the children see God as speechless as stone. When they look to heaven, they see "Dark, wheel-like, turning clouds" as impersonal and dehumanized as those they work with below. And well they might, as Elizabeth states it; for they have never seen sunshine or glory. They know grief without wisdom, are slaves and martyrs without the hope of Christian salvation. And in the final lines Miss Barrett puts the blame squarely where it belongs—on the men and the society that have permitted this brutality to exist.

> "How long," they say, "how long, O cruel nation,
> Will you stand, to move the world, on a child's heart,—
> Stifle down with a mailed heel its palpitation,
> And tread onward to your throne amid the mart?
> Our blood splashes upward, O gold-heaper,
> And your purple shows your path!
> But the child's sob in silence curses deeper
> Than the strong man in his wrath."
>
> (ll. 153–60)

The utilization of her chosen colors of purple and gold, which, as we have seen, are typical when she describes either God or love, lends an irony here when set against the conditions wrought by those "dark, satanic mills." "The Cry of the Children" is a poem which still crops up from time to time in anthologies. It is a good choice, for it remains one of Elizabeth's most effective poems.

V   "Wine of Cyprus"

As we have seen, the blind Classics scholar, Hugh S. Boyd, held no brief for modern literature. And "modern" to him meant anything from the Middle Ages forward. The ballads of Elizabeth Barrett, the poems utilizing the contemporary scene, he found awkward at best and detestable at worst. Chiefly to please this old and very dear friend of hers, she wrote the poem "Wine of Cyprus," [23] in recognition of the gifts of Cyprus wine bestowed upon her from time to time by Boyd. The fact that she herself hated the sweet wine and that her father called it "most beastly and nauseous" [24] did not detract from the generous thought which prompted the gifts and provided the inspiration for the poem.

"Wine of Cyprus" is, as we might expect, full of allusion to the gods and goddesses of Classical antiquity. There is in it a rollicking tone of lusty paganism that reflects the joy she found in her study of the

Classics. At the same time, she recognizes the difference between
Classical libations and Victorian sipping that delineates the essential
differences of the two ages. She has fun with the opening tongue-in-
cheek stanzas quoted below:

I

If old Bacchus were the speaker,
    He would tell you with a sigh
Of the Cyprus in this beaker
    I am sipping like a fly,—
Like a fly or gnat on Ida
    At the hour of goblet-pledge,
By queen Juno brushed aside, a
    Full white arm-sweep, from the edge.

II

Sooth, the drinking should be ampler
    When the drink is so divine,
And some deep-mouthed Greek exemplar
    Would become your Cyprus wine:
Cyclops' mouth might plunge aright in,
    While his one eye overleered,
Nor too large were mouth of Titan
    Drinking rivers down his beard.

(ll. 1—16)

The poem is, in fact, a celebration of the works she had read with
Boyd: Plato, Sophocles, Aeschylus, and the Greek Christian Fathers.
But it is also more than this, for she slyly interjects the idea that she
cannot answer the old thinkers today in the same forms they employed
yesterday: she must sing her song in a form as appropriate as they sang
theirs. The poem is, however, good-humored; appreciative of Boyd's
efforts; and deeply thankful for the joy she has found in her studies
with him. She closes with the thought that, while she may sip from the
wine of Cyprus, she has drunk deep from the Pierian spring, thanks
both to her mentor and to her own insatiable inclination to do so.

VI *"The Dead Pan"*

"Wine of Cyprus," while purer Greek than her poem "The Dead
Pan," [25] is not so interesting; for inspired no doubt by John Kenyon's
translation of Schiller's poem "The Gods of Greece," the poem

urgently forces upon us her attitude that the death of Pan, signalling the death of false gods everywhere, occurred as legend has it when Christ died on the Cross. In her poem, she makes it clear that the death of the false gods of antiquity heralded the revelation of truth in the form of Christianity. She urges her fellow poets to look to the sun, to the light of Christ, for motifs, and to forsake the Classical, mythological figures who died at the death of Pan:

> O brave poets, keep back nothing,
> Nor mix falsehood with the whole!
> Look up Godward; speak the truth in
> Worthy song from earnest soul:
> Hold, in high poetic duty,
> Truest Truth the fairest Beauty!
>   Pan, Pan is dead.
>   (ll. 267—73)

Significantly, however, her best lines occur when she speaks of the gods of Hellas and not when she pontificates (as she does above) about the glories of Christ's sacrifice. When she speaks of Pallas' broad blue eyes, Aphrodite's charms, and of Apollo with his floating golden hair, we are much more intrigued with the ancient beauty sparked by her imagination than we are by the drab commentary on Christian truth. Even when she castigates them for being false gods, we are caught up by the picture of her as a whirling Victorian dervish dashing the chalice to the dust:

> O ye vain false gods of Hellas,
> Ye are silent evermore!
> And I dash down this old chalice
> Whence libations ran of yore,
> See, the wine crawls in the dust
> Wormlike—as your glories must,
>   Since Pan is dead.
>   (ll. 211—17)

When Kenyon criticized her for mentioning the Christian God in the midst of the pagan-god catalogue, she retorted that she would rather be, like Wordsworth, a pagan than a luke warm Christian. She felt it essential to bring Christ into "The Dead Pan," even though the mention detracted from the passionately Platonic tone of the poem. For her, however, "The Christian religion is true or it is not, and if it is true it offers the highest and purest objects of contemplation."[26] Believing sincerely, she had no choice but to castigate the false gods; but by so doing she did, nonetheless, detract from the poem's central tonal emphasis. As her editors, Miss Clarke and Miss Porter, point out, the vigor of the poem arises from her conviction that modern art and literature should take their impetus from contemporary thought and life and thereby let the idols of the past (in this instance, the false gods) be truly dead.[27]

VII   *"Bertha in the Lane"*

Of the other poems in the volumes of 1844, there is not a great deal to say. One, with the ugly title "Bertha in The Lane," [28] tells the sad story of an elder sister, Bertha, who has reared a younger sister after the death of their mother. A young man, who has pledged his love to Bertha, has then seen the younger sister and fallen in love with her; and Bertha obligingly releases him by dying. The poem consists of Bertha's exercise in nobility when she tells her sister that all is forgiven; she may have the young man, for Bertha goes in sweet sacrifice to join their mother, who is in heaven with God. The poem moves along in relatively smooth tetrameter lines, a testimony of Elizabeth's ability to rhyme whenever she so desired. Popular in its day,[29] and exceedingly so with Robert Browning,[30] the poet herself was not particularly impressed with it. As she remarked to Boyd, the poem contains a story which brought tears to a lawyer's cheeks. The people cared for it, but she was well aware that more sophisticated readers such as Boyd would find it nothing but a bore.[31]

VIII   *"The Rhyme of the Duchess May"*

The same might be said for "The Rhyme of the Duchess May," [32] except that it relates a rousing good story with enough dramatic scenes to catch the more sophisticated reader. In the poem, the Duchess May, who is beautiful and who has "muckle gold," has been betrothed as a child to the Lord of Leigh. Since she does not love him, she refuses to marry him and selects instead Guy, Lord of Linteged. After the lovers' escape on a red-roan horse to Linteged, their castle is besieged by the Lord of Leigh—a typical villain, thin of lip and with gnashing white teeth—who is determined to capture the Duchess May and to kill her husband, Guy of Linteged. But the Lord of Linteged, an honorable man, wishes to save his sister and younger brothers from sacrifice; and, knowing that the besieged castle is soon to fall, he orders his horse brought to the ramparts of the castle where he intends to take his last

ride—a long one through the air and hundreds of feet down into the
moat! He intends the Duchess May to know nothing of this sacrifice,
thus he will exonerate his relatives at the expense of his life and for her,
after he is dead, to return to the seat of the Leighs.

When she discovers his plan, she leads the horse to the ramparts; and,
as he mounts the horse, she grabs his stirrup and refuses to release it,
despite his pleading that she do so: "Back he reined the steed—back,
back! but she trailed along his track/ with a frantic clasp and strain" (ll.
359—60). While he tries again and again to dislodge her, the foe clatters
up the steps. She leaps into the saddle too, and the horse rears mightily
and topples; "Then back-toppling, crashing back—a dead wright flung
out to wrack,/ Horse and riders overfell" (ll. 402—3). The action and
drama of the tale are suspended, as is the case with many ballads, by a
gentle refrain: "Oh, the little birds sang east, and the little birds sang
west"—peculiarly affecting when juxtaposed with such violent action.
"The Rhyme of the Duchess May," as we might expect, also received
much acclaim from the public, and it too was a favorite of Robert
Browning. But it was detested by H. S. Boyd, as were most of the
poems of its kind in the 1844 volumes. Times seem to have changed
indeed, for Miss Hayter sees all of the ballads as analogous in
superficiality to the castle on the window blind which confronted
Elizabeth's gaze in the dark bedroom at Wimpole Street,[33] but to
Edmund Stedman, popular American editor, in 1875 the ballads of
Elizabeth Barrett were like Keats's magic casements opening on perilous
seas in fairy lands forlorn![34]

IX *"A Drama of Exile"*

The work Elizabeth Barrett considered the *magnum opus* of the
Poems of 1844 was "A Drama of Exile."[35] Unfortunately, the very
length of the poetic drama (2,270 lines) prohibits its extensive
treatment in this study. We are told that almost no one (and this
included her dearest friends) liked "A Drama of Exile."[36] Critics
found it lacking in unity, coherence, and emphasis, and they pro-
nounced it a dismal failure. In her attempt to portray the experiences
and sorrows of Adam and Eve as they wended their solitary way out of
Eden, she chose a theme less tenuous but scarcely more comprehensible
than that of "The Seraphim." While Mr. Taplin states that the poem
reads like "a burlesque of Paradise Lost,"[37] Miss Hayter flatly declares
that "There is certainly not the least reverberation of Milton in that
extraordinary and unequal work, *A Drama of Exile*."[38] Faced with

such contradictory statements by two highly respected scholars, we are forced to conclude, after looking directly at the poem, that the theme is Miltonic by association only. The themes of alienation and exile, common to *Paradise Lost* on a cosmic scale, are more humanly oriented in "A Drama of Exile." As Elizabeth states in her preface to the poem, Milton was to remain within Eden with his Adam and Eve, unfallen or falling; but she would remain without Eden with the Exiles, herself an exile, thus representative of the human condition as we know it.[39] But she cannot sustain her position, she admits, for she finds herself within the gates of Paradise.

To her credit, and a further testimony of her critical ability, she anticipated the criticism the poem would meet. She knew it would be called derivative and that Milton would be cited as her source. Of this she said, "The Agamemnon of Aeschylus, who died in the bath, did no harm to, nor suffered any harm from, the Agamemnon of Homer who bearded Achilles."[40] That Milton's subject and hers have the same source does not make it follow that the two works are similar or similarly conceived. She also knew that her figure of Christ, transfigured and speaking in a vision to the exiled Adam and Eve, would bring criticism upon her. Here she eloquently defends, as we have seen her defend to Kenyon in "The Dead Pan,"[41] her contention that God and Christ should be household words to men today: they should not be exalted and, in fact, exiled to some Olympian height far removed from human reach and understanding. On this point, she writes in her preface:

There is a feeling abroad which appears to me . . . nearer to superstition than to religion, that there should be no touching of holy vessels except by consecrated fingers, nor any naming of holy names except in consecrated places. As if life were not a continual sacrament to man, since Christ brake daily bread of it in His hands! As if the name of God did not build a church, by the very naming of it! As if the word God were not, everywhere in His creation, and at every moment in His eternity, an appropriate word!

(II, 146)

In general, however, "A Drama of Exile" is a failure, as the critics contended. In spite of her courage, Elizabeth simply could not bring it off successfully. We tire of Eve as Edgar Allan Poe tired of her in his critique of the poem,[42] for she is vaguely constructed, nebulous in intent, shadowy, and unsubstantial.

X *"The Soul's Expression"*

We are happier with the ballads and lyrics included in the *Poems* of 1844 than we are with "A Drama of Exile." In conclusion, we might point out only a few sonnets which remain, and which achieve by their compression the kind of effect never seen in Miss Barrett's long poems. Two, addressed to George Sand, mirror Elizabeth's admiration for her. In one, the oft-quoted "The Soul's Expression," we find accurate self-criticism in its opening lines:

> With stammering lips and insufficient sound
> I strive and struggle to deliver right
> That music of my nature, day and night
> With dream and thought and feeling interwound,
> And inly answering all the senses round
> With octaves of a mystic depth and height
> Which step out grandly to the infinite
> From the dark edges of the sensual ground.
> This song of soul I struggle to outbear
> Through portals of the sense, sublime and whole,
> And utter all myself into the air:
> But if I did it,—as the thunder-roll
> Breaks its own cloud, my flesh would perish there,
> Before that dread apocalypse of soul.

This fine sonnet, quoted in its entirety, shows the perfect integration of thought and form of which Elizabeth was capable when she put her best talents to work.

Of her early work, the poems of 1838 and of 1844, much has been made of Elizabeth's flaws: her lack of compression, her spasmodic tendencies, her obscurity, her use of archaic words, her double rhymes, and her marred rhyme schemes (for there is a possibility that she lisped or never heard the words she used and therefore did not know how to pronounce them). Commentary on all these phases of her work abounds in the early Kenyon *Letters,* in Alethea Hayter's study, in Gardner Taplin's study, as well as in contemporary reviews of her poetry. It is generally conceded, however, that she improved in all these respects and that this improvement can most readily be seen in the *Poems* of 1850—the first collected edition containing almost all her earlier poems written from 1838 on, in the *Sonnets from the Portuguese,* and in her series of political poems. When we turn to a consideration of those poems in the edition of 1850 which we have not already examined, we shall see that the critics are justified in their judgment that Elizabeth had seen fit to cull and prune the defects from her poetry. But, before we discuss these revised, polished, and added-to poems, it would be well to look at her prose, both as repository for her criticism and for the illumination it provides for our view of her fine *Sonnets from the Portuguese*. Furthermore, the prose indicates her development both intellectually and emotionally into the mature woman and artist she was destined to become.

CHAPTER 5

The Prose: The Artist in Letters

I NSIGHT into Elizabeth Barrett's personal relationships, while important if we are to know her thoroughly, is not all that her letters grant us. As a critic, she is generally given short shrift; but this should not be the case, for, in her comments on individual works and on poets whom she knew, she demonstrates again that she knows, for the most part, whereof she speaks. Her ability to be astute and incisive as a critic is clearly demonstrable, even though the bulk of her criticism is contained within letters. This chapter not only indicates such critical acuity but also serves as an introduction to her *Sonnets from the Portuguese* insofar as it treats of her interpersonal relationships (with family, friends, and associates) as reflected in her letters.

As a letter writer, Elizabeth Barrett was an excellent stylist whose pen moved skillfully, with wit, charm, and astuteness; her letters fill at least eight volumes, with more still to be edited. That amazing faculty that some writers have for knowing the individual reader—his idiosyncrasies, hopes, dreams, attitudes—belonged to her when she wrote a letter. For example, the letters to her sister Henrietta, written after her marriage to Robert Browning, are full of the details of her domestic life in Italy: the scenery and countryside; the daily menus; their visitors; Robert's consideration for her; their habits and habitations; her baby son, his frolics and foibles; their servants; their trips; and, above all, testimonies of her love for her sister, for her husband, for her son, and for beautiful, restorative Italy. That Henrietta, by this time Mrs. Surtees Cook, a married woman with three children but once Ba's closest sister, would have interests quite different from Elizabeth's old friend, Miss Mitford, was a fact Mrs. Browning knew quite well.

Because of this recognition, the letters (written before as well as after her marriage to Browning) to Miss Mitford, critic, woman of letters, and raconteur, strike a very different note. In these, Elizabeth speaks of the contemporary writing of the day, of politics, of mutual friends, of her inmost thoughts, and, of course, of Flush—the spaniel that Miss Mitford had given her and who had accompanied her to Italy. The letters to Hugh Boyd, the blind poet and Classicist, are still more technical. Long discussions of prosody, of the early Greek Christian poets, of poetry, and of the reviews—of her own poetry and of others'—fill the volume edited by Professor McCarthy. On the other hand, Boyd was also an old and very dear friend, and so there are letters illustrative of her great affection for him. He, after all, divined that she would marry Robert Browning before any but her sisters knew of it. Not only did she confess the secret to him, but she also went to his house directly after her wedding in Marylebone Church.[1]

Because of the dual role he played, we read the following of her words to him and know that he is one of the few qualified to help her with her translation of the Greek Christian Fathers: "Chrysostom has been staggering me lately by his commentary on those passages of the Epistles to the Corinthians, which relate to the Lord's supper. I have felt every now and then, that he *must* hold transubstantiation,—and then I look at your pencil marks upon those very passages, and recollect your opinion of his holding no such doctrine—and then I am in perplexity, and wonder how you can possibly reconcile some of his expressions with your opinion." [2]

I *The Critic's Stance*

In addition to being interesting stylistically, the letters to Boyd, to Miss Mitford, and to Robert Browning in Volume I of the *Love Letters* form a rich repository for Elizabeth's critical commentary. In letters to these literary friends she comments about writers of both past and present. Ranging from her interest in the esoteric writers of the past to the more viable writers of the Victorian present, she has something of value to say about nearly everyone.

As indicated previously, her early letters to Boyd are full of discussion concerning her preparation of four papers for publication in the *Athenaeum* on the Greek Christian Fathers: Chrysostom, Gregory, Basil, and Synesius. She has been avidly studying Greek with Boyd in order to effect proper reading; but, at the same time, she was also reading Hebrew. These letters are filled with her comments about the "ancients"—Homer, Plato, Lucretius, Lucan, Aeschylus, Virgil, Catullus, Sophocles, Longinus, Euripides—and also about such "moderns" as Boyd would tolerate: Ben Jonson, Shakespeare, Milton, Francis Bacon, Alexander Pope. The philosophers Locke, Hume, and Berkeley also beg her attention; of these men she has this to say: "I

neither doubt his conscientiousness, nor am surprised at his con-
clusions—for, rejecting, as he did, the testimony of his eyes and
ears,—he could not be expected to receive that of his reason." [3] As this
comment indicates, all was not a dream world to her; she could be both
practical and tart in a critical sense.

A considerable amount of her energies were directed to a defense of
the Romantics. Mr. Boyd was most unsympathetic not only to
"modern" literature but, in particular, to Wordsworth, whom he
regarded as third-rate, to the exasperation of Elizabeth, who wrote to
Miss Mitford, saying: "[Mr. Boyd] and I must talk and agree in Greek
alone for the remainder of our lives." [4] But she does not surrender to
Boyd in the argument over Wordsworth's merits; for, in 1842, where
she sent her article on the poet to Boyd, she remarked that he is not
"obliged" to read it, but, at the same time, she is not "obliged" to
believe what he says about Wordsworth. She writes: "Pope—Goldsmith!
Measure out broad praises to either!—but for genius, for philosophy, for
various and expressive language and cadence,—for *poetry,* in brief—you
cannot seriously place Wordsworth below *them*. Oh surely, surely
not!" [5]

Nor does the argument hover over Wordsworth only, for it extends
to include a discussion of the comparative merits of Wordsworth,
Coleridge, and Byron. Elizabeth demonstrates that she is not destruc-
tively judicial in her criticisms but that she is appreciative of the best
efforts of each of the poets:

You cannot praise Byron as a poet, with warmer words than are always
ready for him on my lips; he was a great and wonderful poet—
passionate—eloquent—witty—with all powers of swift allusion and
sarcasm and satire—full and rapid in the mechanical resources of his art,
and capable of a sufficient and brilliant conveyance of philosophic
thought and argument. In many, in most of these points he is superior
beyond all comparison to Wordsworth—who is not passionate—nor
witty—nor sarcastic—nor satirical—nor brilliant—nor particularly
flexible and facile in rhyme and rhythm. Still I am not, in my own
view, guilty of inconsistency, when I hold that Wordsworth is the
greater poet in the proper sense of greatness, the profounder thinker,
the nearer to poetic secrets of nature, more universal, more elevated,
more full and consistent in his own poetic individuality,—and more
influential for good upon the literature of his country and age.[6]

In general, Wordsworth is today assigned a higher rank than Byron,
chiefly because no one has ever called into question his sincerity. With

the exception of the satirical verse, much of Byron now appears dated and overly emotional; but the high seriousness of "Tintern Abbey," the "Immortality Ode," and vast sections of the *Prelude* rings as true for us today as it did for the young Elizabeth.

Even more astute than her comment about Byron and Wordsworth is her judgment of Coleridge, as the recent criticism of Coleridge confirms. "The Rime of the Ancient Mariner" she judges with undeniable contemporaneity, saying that the poem "is one of its kind,—most singular and supreme in dauntless originality and sublime conception—the work of a soul more intensely poetical (in the appreciation of mind) than either the author of the Excursion or he of Childe Harold." [7] As for the younger Romantics, Keats and Shelley,— they also held her admiration. When Boyd wrote to her that there was one poet she had never praised, she replied: "Why who can *he* be? Did you never hear me praise *Shelley*? Can it be *Shelley*? What you say of the cadencial music might perfectly apply to him—and he was very capable of the pathetic, altho' he did not keep near enough to Humanity to communicate largely and warmly with its emotions." [8]

To Miss Mitford, however, she confides that she finds Shelley's spiraling pursuit of the gleam a more serious fault: "It was Shelley that high, and yet too low, elemental poet, who froze in cold glory between Heaven and earth, neither dealing with man's heart, beneath, nor aspiring to communion with the supernal Humanity, the heart of the God-Man. Therefore his poetry glitters and is cold—and it is only by momentary stirrings that we can discern the power of sweet human love and deep pathos which was in *him* and should have been in *it*." [9] Very likely, this comment is a more accurate estimate of her critical evaluation of Shelley than is the one made to Boyd because she seeks to offset the prejudice he displays toward the "moderns" by softening her criticism.

She has less to say about Keats than about any other of the Romantics; but what she does say, is laudatory. In a letter to Miss Mitford she calls Keats a "true true poet, from his first words to his last, when he said he 'felt the daisies growing over him.' " [10] She then quotes her friend and collaborator, Mr. Horne, who did not believe that the critics killed Keats (as did many, including Byron) and said, "He was already bending over his grave in sweet and solemn contemplation, when the satyrs *hoofed* him into it." [11]

Her evaluation of the Romantics remains sound: Coleridge is cited for his unique grasp of mind; Wordsworth, for his high seriousness; Byron, for his wit; Shelley, for his musical though esoteric verse; and

Keats for his sweetly plaintive longing for the end, a Jove recognized by his Thunder.[12]

Her estimate of the great Victorians is no less accurate and valuable. She knows the age, its attitudes, its frustrations, its hopes, its fears. All the more remarkable is the fact that she was one of the few to recognize early in his career the genius of Robert Browning, who as a young and aspiring poet was anathema to critics and readers alike. Of the three Victorians whom she chose to elevate highest he was one; Tennyson and Carlyle are the others.

Her uncompromising defense of Browning began before she ever met him. She was well aware of his faults, as the following excerpts illustrate; but she was one of the very few to mark his virtues. In an early letter to Miss Mitford on the subject of Browning's poem "Paracelsus," she notes his lack of clarity and compression; but she adds: "I do think and feel that the pulse of poetry is full and warm and strong in it ... I wish you would read it and agree with me that the author is a poet in the holy sense." [13] But Miss Mitford finds it difficult to agree in the matter of Robert Browning's genius, for she believed him to be foppish, effeminate, obscure, and dilatory.[14] This attitude was to prevail and to provoke from Elizabeth additional and equally incisive critical commentary on the poet. Over and over again she stresses that Browning is "no imitator" and that, though he lacks "music," she is impressed with his "strong and deep individuality." [15]

Four years before Elizabeth met Browning, she wrote a spirited commentary to Miss Mitford on "Pippa Passes" and "Paracelsus:"

I like, I do like the "heart of a mystery" when it beats moderate time. I like a twilight of mysticism—when the sun and moon both shine together. Yes—and I like "Pippa" too. There are fine things in it—and the presence of genius, never to be denied! At the same time it is hard ... to understand—isn't it? Too hard? I think so! And the fault of Paracelsus,—the defect in harmony, is here too. After all, Browning is a true poet—and there are not many such poets—and if any critics have, as your critical friend wrote to you, "flattered him into a wilderness and left him" they left him alone with his genius—and where those two are, despair cannot be. The wilderness will blossom soon, with a brighter rose than "Pippa." [16]

And, of course, the wilderness did blossom with a good many roses brighter than "Pippa;" it is to Elizabeth's credit that she had the critical insight to predict that this would be so.

Neither is she blind to Browning's talent as dramatist; she, herself, praises his dramatic efforts. But she also says that he would be better off to stick with poetry, for the "great unwashed" audience of theatergoers does not appreciate the subtleties inherent in his dramas.[17] For his play *A Blot on the Scutcheon* she has nothing but praise, saying that, for her, "he is a master in clenched passion, . . . concentrated passion . . . burning through the metallic fissures of language."[18] If that "concentrated passion" is somewhat obscure where the mass of men are concerned, Elizabeth is not at all discouraged; for she recognizes a kinship of obscurity with Browning.

Her criticism of Browning's works became even more accurate after they had met and talked. Daily letters kept her abreast of his literary endeavors, and she rose to be helpful to him. In a very early letter, dated January 15, 1845, she centered on the quintessence of Robert Browning's talent: "You have in your vision two worlds, or to use the language of the schools of the day, you are both subjective and objective in the habits of your mind. You can deal both with abstract thought and with human passion in the most passionate sense. Thus, you have an immense grasp in Art; and no one at all accustomed to consider the usual forms of it, could help regarding with reverence and gladness the gradual expansion of your powers."[19]

In a well-known, early letter, Browning has written the following to her: "You speak out, *you,*—I only make men and women speak—give you truth broken into prismatic hues, and fear the pure white light, even if it is in me, but I am going to try; so it will be no small comfort to have your company just now, seeing that when you have your men and women aforesaid, you are busied with them, whereas it seems bleak, melancholy work, this talking to the wind. . . ."[20] Elizabeth's reply, cited in the preceding quotation, shows her appreciation for his dual ability. He not only "speaks out himself" but also speaks through his created characters; therefore, Robert Browning is both subjective and objective as poet; and his future wife had the critical sense to recognize that this was so. While contemporary Browning scholarship has long looked upon Browning as an "objective" poet, there is a recent tendency to temper this opinion, thereby bringing the consensus more into line with the view held by Miss Barrett. Early in the *Love Letters* she assesses his potential and tells him that he has not yet written the greatest of his poems. What he has accomplished by 1845 she expresses with clarity:

You have thrown out fragments of *os* . . . *sublime* . . . indicative of soul-mammothism—and you live to develop your nature,—if you live.

That is easy and plain. You have taken a great range—from those high faint notes of the mystics which are beyond personality . . . to dramatic impersonations, gruff with nature . . . and when these are thrown into harmony, as in a manner they are in "Pippa Passes" . . . the combinations of effect must always be striking and noble—and you must feel yourself drawn on to such combinations more and more.[21]

She was until the very end of her life to regard Robert Browning as a superior poet, as a man of genius—perhaps the greatest measure of her critical acumen. She knew quality, and she never had the slightest question in her mind about the poetic power of Robert Browning. The following excerpt from a letter to Sarianna Browning, written by Elizabeth in 1860, illustrates her tenacious way of bolstering her husband:

Ah! dear Sarianna, I don't complain for myself of an unappreciating public—I *have no reason*. But, just for *that* reason, I complain more about Robert, only he does not hear me complain. To *you* I may say, that the blindness, deafness, and stupidity of the English public to Robert are amazing. Of course Milsand had "heard his name"! Well, the contrary would have been strange. Robert *is*. All England can't prevent his existence, I suppose. But nobody there, except a small knot of pre-Raffaelite *[sic]* men, pretend to do him justice.[22]

Although she lauded Robert Browning as man and poet to the end of her life, her letters abound in astute criticism of his various poems and of his dramas. The extent to which she influenced the poetry of Robert Browning may never be assessed, but it is certainly reasonable to conclude that he might have quit writing poetry had he not had her unflagging moral support.

After Browning, her praise redounds upon Tennyson. In one of the *Love Letters* she asks if Browning knows him face to face.[23] She expresses great admiration for Tennyson, saying, "In execution, he is exquisite,—and, in music, a most subtle weigher out to the ear of fine airs."[24] Of Tennyson's *Poems in Two Volumes* she writes enthusiastically to Miss Mitford that they have wrapped her in Elysium.[25] In this same letter she notes that Tennyson has improved his style: there is "less of quaint peculiarity, more individuality, more *power* . . . , more thought under the obvious literary forms, and *less* of that high ideality which distinguished the Old Tennyson lyrics."[26] Of "Locksley Hall" she writes to Miss Mitford of her dislike for Amy, an insipid, shallow, snobbish, and foolish heroine. This is, of course, exactly as Tennyson intended Amy to be seen through the rejected hero's eyes. When Miss Mitford conveyed Leigh Hunt's criticism that Tennyson was too "sensual," Elizabeth wrote in reply: "He has not flesh and blood enough to be sensual—his forms are too obviously on the surface to wear pulses." [27]

Certainly, Elizabeth is a Romantic critic, more impressionistic than analytic, and consequently very often quite happy to follow the dramatic lead of the poet under consideration. It is refreshing to read once again a critic who dares to become involved, for so much of modern criticism strikes us as belonging to the dissection room; indeed, we even surgically entitle criticism from time to time: *Anatomy of Criticism* by Northrup Frye. Elizabeth's wry remarks about Tennyson's *The Princess,* however, illustrate that she predicted the poem might well be what it really was, a noble failure. She writes to Robert Browning: "[Tennyson] has finished the second book . . . and it is in blank verse and a fairy tale, and called the 'University,' the university-members being all females . . . I don't know what to think—it makes me open my eyes. Now isn't this world too old and fond of steam, for blank verse poems, in ever so many books, to be written on the fairies?" [28] Nonetheless, she remained an admirer of Tennyson to the end of her life and, furthermore, became (along with her husband) the Laureate's devoted friend.

The third of her most esteemed Victorians, Carlyle, enjoys her equally accurate appraisal. In reply to Miss Mitford's statement that Carlyle did not write "pure English," Elizabeth responds: "He does not write pure English—no, nor quite pure German—nor pure Greek, by any means. But he writes *thoughts.*" [29] She seizes on Carlyle's special gift, calling him "a great prose poet" and, therefore, worthy of all poets' praise. With precision she notes the distinguishing characteristics of Carlyle's apocalyptic style: "There is something wonderful in this struggling forth into sound of a contemplation bred high above dictionaries and talkers—in some silent Heavenly place for the mystic and true. The sounds do come—strangely indeed and in unwrought masses, but still with a certain confused music and violent eloquence, which prove the power of *thought* over *sound.*" [30] Her opinion, which she elaborates in a letter to Browning, is that Carlyle is "a poet unaware of himself" who lacks only "the sense of music." [31] Her one quarrel with Carlyle lay, of course, in his insistence that the actions of men of history were greater than the actions of poets. She reacts strongly against this contention, writing tartly to Robert: "As if Shakespeare's actions were not greater than Cromwell's!" [32]

Again, as with her criticism of the Romantics, Elizabeth skillfully pinpoints the outstanding merits of the great Victorians: Browning's modernity, implicit in his originality and the pulsing vitality of his dramatic talent; Tennyson's sweet music and superior metrical ability; Carlyle's apocalyptic and poetic prose, resounding from a Victorian Golgotha.

But she did not confine her critical comments to the English scene, for she notes the provincialism of American literature, in a letter to Miss Mitford and wonders why this should be so.[33] Of James Russell Lowell, she writes to Browning that, while Lowell is respectable for an American critic, he actually knows nothing at all about English poetry.[34] Her critical comments about German literature are few, but she does state that she reveres and loves Goethe more than Schiller because Goethe "did not . . . neglect the humanities, in their strict human sense."[35] However, it is in the area of French literature that Elizabeth waxes long and eloquent. She had always been addicted to French novels, and she knew the novelists through her familiarity with their work. Many of those she praised are virtually unknown to us today: Eugène Sue, Frédéric Soulié, and Louis de Maynard de Queilhe; but her favorites remain important: Victor Hugo, Honoré de Balzac, and George Sand. In general, she finds French literature "Full of power and caprice and extravagance."[36] The one flaw rests in its want of "fixed principle." French novels are fiery and exciting while, she writes, English novels tend to be "dull and cold."[37]

She ranks the great French triumvirate in this order: Sand, Hugo, and Balzac. The years have not proved Elizabeth's estimate to be right; however, she demonstrates that she knows her own prejudice when she writes to Miss Mitford: "Victor Hugo stands first of all in genius . . . if I could make up my mind to call George Sand *second* to any genius living."[38] Such judgment is pure prejudice, but it is interesting because it illuminates Elizabeth's many-sided personality. George Sand was a Romantic, a cigar-smoking transvestite who fooled the public with her perfectly conventional unconventional love affairs. Her novels were risqué and, for the period, frankly so. Elizabeth Barrett was both attracted and repelled by her; for, to her, George Sand is a "wonderful genius . . . *shameless* as she is sometimes."[39] While Elizabeth deplores the fact that Sand aggrandizes the "physical aspect of passion," she writes admiringly that "she is eloquent as a fallen angel."[40] The sensational novel *Leila* made Elizabeth blush and state: "Who could hold such a book for five minutes in one hand while a coal-fire burnt within reach of the other"; yet she found another work, *Les Maîtres*

Mosaïstes, fit for any governess to read to her pupils.[41] *Leila* held her nonetheless: it was "a serpent book both for language-color and soul-shame."[42] *Indiana* was "less revolting as a whole" but was also sensual and physical. It was to *Leila,* however, that she turned her comments again and again.

We might wonder why the supposedly sheltered Elizabeth Barrett Browning would be so attracted to this aspect of George Sand's work. We need not concern ourselves unduly, however, because Elizabeth herself would, in the future, write a verse-novel, *Aurora Leigh,* which would shock Victorian mothers to the point of forbidding their daughters to read it. A kind of reluctant admiration for George Sand held Elizabeth well past her marriage to Robert Browning; and then the story of her meeting with George Sand is an amusing one. She and her husband, while in Paris, sought and obtained an audience. To the consternation of Robert, the French author was surrounded by young male sycophants who spat, smoked, and worshiped at the rather portly woman's feet. Elizabeth maintained her equilibrium throughout the interview drawn as she always was by the androgynous quality of George Sand.[43] To Robert Browning she had elucidated this idea in an early letter (1845), when she wrote of the comparative merits of men versus women:

... I believe women ... all of us in a mass ... to have minds of quicker movement, but less power and depth ... and that we are under your feet, because we can't stand upon our own. ... One woman indeed now alive ... and only *that* one down all the ages of the world—seems to me to justify for a moment an opposite opinion—that wonderful woman George Sand; who has something monstrous in combination with her genius. ... Such a colossal nature in every way,—with all that breadth and scope of faculty which women want—magnanimous, and loving the truth and loving the people—and with that "hate of hate" too, which you extol—so eloquent, and yet earnest as if she were dumb—so full of a living sense of beauty, and of noble blind instincts towards an ideal purity—and so proving a right even in her wrong.[44]

Elizabeth Barrett's attitude toward George Sand had, in one sense, its counterpart in her attitude toward Robert Browning. She liked a woman who had both masculine and feminine qualities of mind, and she married a man who had similar androgynous qualities. By way of proof is her defense of Robert, whom Miss Mitford had attacked as being "effeminate." She writes obliquely: "Coleridge said, that every great man he ever knew, had something of the woman in him with one exception: and the exception was Wordsworth. Now mind! The observation was intended as no reproach to great men generally, but praise—and the subject defined had no relation to *effeminacy* (strictly speaking) but to softness . . . tenderness! So I in my perversity, put your remark and Coleridge's together, or rather plunge yours into Coleridge's and leave it there liquidated!" [45]

While we have no time for a discussion of the psychological makeup of either Elizabeth or Robert Browning, it is worth noting that the excerpts may form a basis for judging Elizabeth's general approach to both George Sand and Robert Browning. Furthermore, such an approach might well be used as an antidote to Professor Miller's psychological study in which Robert is portrayed as a man who puts his wife on a pedestal as he had similarly elevated his mother.[46] Androgynous qualities of mind in a writer are more apt to enhance his or her writing than to detract from it, as Virginia Woolf so eloquently expressed in her essay "A Room of One's Own." [47]

About her own abilities and limitations as a writer, Elizabeth was not only objective but sound. To Miss Mitford she wrote: "I am afraid I am very apt not to speak plain when I write." [48] Her father had been one of the earliest to note her lack of clarity and subsequent critical commentaries have made the same point. In explaining her problem to Robert Browning, she tells him that it is her nature to rush "headlong" into things. She realizes that such impulsiveness will not do for a writer, and she states that she has long tried to discipline herself. She knows that she has been charged by critics with saying everything she thinks—with being overly effusive and "spasmodic." She recognizes the great chasm between the things she says and those she would say, but her will to overcome the disparity is strong enough to spur her on. On one point she disagrees with her critics: "I do not *say everything I think*— but I *take every means to say what I think,* which is different." [49]

We have reviewed her juvenilia and found them wanting, but typically so; for that is the way of juvenilia. Of her own early poems she writes that Coleridge's daughter was correct in referring to her *Essay on Mind* as "a mere 'girl's exercise'; because it is just *that* and no more. . . ." [50] She knows that the poem does not reflect her nature, that it tends to be pedantic; but she also knows that early poems are generally poor. She also states that her life as a recluse in the years before Browning has not helped her to infuse vitality into her writing.[51]

II   *The Personal Voice*

Turning from her critical commentary to her engaging personal letters, we see that, while much of her mind and heart is involved with Robert Browning, much remains for her other friends and relatives. Always she knows the recipient of her letter in such a way that she speaks to his or her individuality. In her letters to her brother George, which stand as a case in point, she tends to tease this ponderous, eternal bachelor who was by occupation a barrister of the Inner Temple. In a letter written while she was resting at Torquay, she says: "God bless and keep you dearest Georgie!—I need not tell you how high and deep you are in my esteem and love—and now that you have not forgotten me on the reception of your first briefs, I rejoice in feeling sure that you won't cut me when you are chancellor." [52] And again, in a letter written from Wimpole Street on December 21, 1843, she closes facetiously with the comment, "Write to me, George—A hundred briefs be with you!" [53]

That Miss Barrett respected this brother greatly, often seeking his advice, cannot be questioned; and one incident that illuminates her respect bears recounting. When Benjamin Haydon committed suicide, he (although he had never met Miss Barrett) assigned all of his personal papers to her. They were delivered to Wimpole Street in a huge trunk, to her great chagrin. Shortly thereafter, Robert Browning attended a dinner party at which an allusion was made to Miss Barrett's having been a "*very* particular friend of Haydon's." [54] In her letter to George, she recounts how Robert Browning had exploded at the implication that she was more than a correspondent of Haydon's and how she had written at once (at Browning's suggestion) to Mr. Talfourd, the executor of Haydon's estate and at whose table the incident had occurred, to ask him what she could do about the situation. She writes to George in the confidence that he will straighten things out with Talfourd, and that he will also be most discreet with reference to her relationship with Browning:

You will observe too that Mr. Browning's account to me of what has passed at Mr. Talfourd's table, is not to be referred to or repeated, anywise or anywhere. . . . I have no claim on *him*, Talfourd—he is not my friend. . . . But I heard all this from Mr. Browning and you must not on any account let it be breathed by other breath than our own. I never saw him [Browning] so angry since our acquaintance began. Worse things were said or implied I do not doubt, than what he told me, he was *so* angry. . . . Have I made it clear to you, George? I have been vexed, perplexed, more than you will fancy perhaps—yet I am sure you will see that it is an unpleasant position. Write your thoughts to me and advise.[55]

Not only does this letter reveal her respect for George, it also reflects her deep concern that the relationship between Browning and herself be kept from the world—as well as from her father. While her sisters were aware by this time of its intensity, her brothers knew only that Mr. Browning was a friend of Ba's and that Ba wanted the fact kept quiet. Later, Elizabeth wrote one of her most poignant letters to George to tell him of her marriage. This letter begins with the words, "I throw myself on your affection for me and beseech of God that it may hold under the weight—," and she continues by asking him to go to his room to read the letter.[56] She then most eloquently describes her love for Browning, his for her, the deepening of this love over the two-year time period of their acquaintance, her reasons for keeping the relationship as secret as possible—reasons which George himself knew well. The letter closes with sincerity, humility, and, above all, honor:

George, believe of me, and I have endeavoured in all this matter to do right according to my own view of rights and righteousness—If it is not your view, bear with me and pardon me. Do you all pardon me, my beloved ones, and believe that if I could have benefitted any of you by staying here, I would have stayed. Have I not done for you what I could, always? *When* I could—Now I am weak. And if in this crisis I were to do otherwise than what I am about to do, there would be a victim without an expiation, and a sacrifice without an object. My spirits would have festered on in this enforced prison, and none of you all would have been the happier for what would have [been] bitter to *me*. Also, I should have wronged *another*. I cannot do it.[57]

That George shared her father's initial feelings upon receipt of the letter puzzles most students of the matter. After the first trip which the Brownings took to England, however, he did relent. There was a reconciliation, and more letters follow. While these later letters to George speak chiefly of politics and requests for legal assistance,[58] they also, in their composite form, help to support the view that she was nobody's fool and, furthermore, that she was highly intelligent and discerning in her knowledge of the world she lived in.

Professor Landis, editor of the letters to George Barrett, has said perhaps all and more that should be said on this subject in his brilliant analysis of the difference between the personalities of Elizabeth Barrett and Robert Browning.[59] The popular myth perpetrated and perpetuated by the Rudolph Besier play, *The Barretts of Wimpole Street,* which holds that the dashing thirty-four-year-old Browning rushed to the aid of the ailing and weak forty-year-old Miss Barrett—sweeping her off her couch and carrying her to the never-never land of health and happiness in Italy—has been demolished by Landis' introductory discussion. He is right when he says that a close scrutiny of the entire corpus of the letters serves to confirm this myth-breaking. On the other hand, the *Love Letters,* edited in two volumes by F. G. Kenyon, stand as a tremendous repository of knowledge about the two poets from 1845 to 1846. They provide us, as much as anything does in prose, with an account of the inner selves of the individuals concerned. And at this moment in time we are, indeed, transported into a romance which truly clouds our objectivity and makes it all too easy to accept myth.

In a prefatory note to the edition of the *Love Letters,* Robert Wiedemann Barrett Browning (Pen) writes as follows: "In considering the question of publishing these letters, which are all that ever passed between my father and mother, for after their marriage they were never separated, it seemed to me that my only alternatives were to allow them to be published or to destroy them. . . . My father destroyed all the rest of his correspondence, and not long before his death he said, referring to these letters: 'There they are, do with them as you please when I am dead and gone!' "[60]

And so Pen published them, this record of the most intense relationship of the nineteenth century. Read in conjunction with the *Sonnets from the Portuguese,* the most significant poetry Elizabeth ever wrote, these letters tell the story of that love in prose. And she stated clearly to Robert Browning that she saw, in retrospect, no reason for biographers to suppress letters of famous persons. In fact, she favored letters as reliable records of the activities of great men and women: "I, for my part, value letters (to talk literature) as the most vital part of biography, and for any rational human being to put his foot on the traditions of his kind in this particular class, does seem to me as wonderful as possible."[61]

The letters, posted almost daily from Browning's home and from 50 Wimpole Street, increase in intensity and intimacy from 1845 to 1846. In his first letter (January 10, 1845), Browning has written impulsively (a characteristic of his letters) to her that he has loved her verses and that he loves her too. He states that, as a fellow craftsman, he really ought to find fault with her work, but that he cannot because: "part of me has it become, this great living poetry of yours. . . ."[62] She acknowledges this letter graciously and thanks him for his kind words about her poetry. Asking him for his criticisms of her work, she then compliments him on his own with the words, "But with my high respect for your power in your Art and for your experience as an artist, it would be quite impossible for me to hear a general observation of yours on what appear to you my master-faults, without being the better for it hereafter in some way." [63]

While the tone of his first letter is vigorous and enthusiastic, its prose falls roughly about our ears. His dash is too often self-conscious; her informal yet gracious conversational tone is never so. When he asks if he might come to call on her, she answers that he may but must wait for spring, because "Winters shut me up as they do a dormouse's eyes; in the spring, *we shall see*: and I am so much better that I seem turning round to the outward world again. And in the meantime I have learnt to know your voice, not merely from the poetry but from the kindness in it." [64] Here we see her caution, her humor, and her charm.

The relationship between them developed rapidly, and long before they were to meet she expressed her pleasure that he would want to write to her: "it would be strange and contradictory if I were not always delighted both to hear from *you* and to write to *you*, this talking on paper being as good a social pleasure as another." [65] And she means what she says, for she wishes to know him as a poet and as a person. She is not interested in observing the conventions of the time, for she asks him to be himself, so that she in turn can be herself: "don't let us have any constraint, and ceremony! *Don't* be civil to me when you feel rude,—nor loquacious when you incline to silence,—nor yielding in the manners when you are perverse in the mind . . . let us rest from the bowing and courtesying, You and I, on each side." [66]

They move from exploring each other's minds to exploring each other's hearts; and, except for one early abortive letter in which Robert declared his intentions to make her his own and she rejected this in her shock that he would say so, the friendship achieves the intensity of a deep love relationship. The letters are full of his visits, for he had finally succeeded in gaining an audience with her in the first days of June, 1845. From then on his visits are, at first, once a week, then twice, and finally almost daily. The house at Wimpole Street was safe for him from three until six in the afternoon; but there were times, many times, when she had to write to say that Miss Mitford, Mr. Kenyon, or numerous aunts and uncles of the family were expected, and that he must postpone his visit for another day. The wonder was that they succeeded at all in getting to know each other in that busy, bustling London household.

One great fear was ever present: that Mr. Barrett would discover their intensity. He knew that Browning visited his daughter; he accepted him as a poet; but that the poet might be loved and be in love with his favorite daughter was a thought too monstrous to have occurred to him! Time and again Elizabeth reiterates her fear of her father's finding them out. These letters so throb with fear that even after more than a hundred years they carry us into the stifling atmosphere of the Wimpole Street house. In a letter dated September 16, 1845, she states that her father "never *does* tolerate in his family (sons or daughters) the development of one class of feelings."[67] And, in a shocking letter of January 18, 1846, she tells how her father has reacted brutally to Henrietta's request for permission to be courted: "Oh, the dreadful scenes! and only because she had seemed to feel a little. I told you, I think, that there was an obliquity—an eccentricity, or something beyond—on one class of subjects. I hear how her knees were made to ring upon the floor, now! she was carried out of the room in strong hysterics, and I, who rose up to follow her, though I was quite well at that time and suffered only by sympathy, fell flat down upon my face in a fainting-fit."[68] We might well wonder what Robert Browning thought of Mr. Barrett when he read such an account, and how he must have felt when Miss Barrett wrote in the same letter: "I hope we *both* are aware that nothing can be more hopeless than our position in some relations and aspects, though you do not guess perhaps that the very approach to the subject is shut up by dangers, and that from the moment of suspicion entering *one* mind [her father's, of course], we should be able to meet never again in this room, nor to have intercourse by letter through the ordinary channel. I mean, that letters of yours, addressed to me here, would infallibly be stopped and destroyed—if not opened."[69] Because of her life in such an atmosphere, we can agree with Professor Landis wholeheartedly when he states: "If, as the commentators are fond of pointing out, Browning saw in Caponsacchi himself rescuing Elizabeth Barrett from the prison of Wimpole Street, he certainly failed to see that all the real courage, physical as well as spiritual, was hers."[70]

There is no question but that the portraits of Elizabeth Barrett and Robert Browning emerge from these letters in sharp detail. She appears, a semi-invalid of forty, wan and pale, addicted to morphine, troubled by the London cold and air which wrought havoc with her weak lungs.

But she also emerges as a gracious, talented, intelligent, and, above all, courageous and sensitive woman. He appears vigorous, aggressive, sentimental, and, when all is said and done, boyish. She is a mature woman; and he, though thirty-four, often seems a very young adult. In his youthful way, he tells her that he would help her to escape from the confines of London, which she has been told by her physician will kill her if she does not go to Pisa in search of a warmer and more temperate climate. But her father has refused to permit her to take a brother or sister with her. She writes in discouragement to Robert: "I had done living, I thought, when you came and sought me out! and why? and to what end? *That* I cannot help thinking now." [71] And he, who had formerly been chastised by her for feeling that he was "in love" with her, writes: "I would marry you now and thus—I would come when you bade me—I would be no more than one of your brothers—'no more'...." [72] While Elizabeth was very likely not interested in having another brother (having had eight, six living), she replies that the letter has touched her, "more profoundly than I thought even *you* could have touched me...." [73]

Out of this impossible situation—a father who would not permit her either to marry or to leave England in search of health—the letters increase in intensity, interspersed with such practical comments as the one she made about her money (she had an income of three to four hundred pounds a year). She writes to Robert: "And is not the chief good of money, the being free from the need of thinking of it? It seems so to me." [74] As 1845 moves into 1846, with still no solution to their dilemma, they make plans to marry and to escape from England. As April, 1846, arrives, the letters become almost achingly physical; for kisses and embraces are recorded, it seems, on every page. [75] But even in April she is her own woman; and she expects him to be his own man, saying: "You are good and kind ... and I love you gratefully and shall to the end ... yet you cannot, you know,—'submit' to me in an *opinion,* anymore than I could to you, if I desired it ever so anxiously." [76]

On September 12, 1846, Robert Browning and his cousin met Elizabeth Barrett and her maid, Wilson, at Marylebone Church in London, two blocks from 50 Wimpole Street; and there they were married. [77] Directly after their marriage, they separated—she to return to Wimpole Street; and he to his home until their flight on Saturday, September 20. The letters during these days are among the most poignant she ever wrote to him. The day after the wedding, Sunday, postmarked September 14, she wrote her husband:

My own beloved, if ever you should have reason to complain of me in things voluntary and possible, all other women would have a right to tread me underfoot, I should be so vile and utterly unworthy. There is my answer to what you wrote yesterday of wishing me to be better to me . . . you! What could be better than lifting me from the ground and carrying me into life and sunshine? I was yours rather by right than by gift (yet by gift also, my beloved!); for what you have saved and renewed is surely yours. All that I am, I owe you—if I enjoy anything now and henceforth, it is through you. You know this well. Even as I, from the beginning, knew that I had no power against you, . . . or that, if I *had*, it was for your sake.[78]

When the boxes had been packed and sent, and she was ready to slip quietly out of the house with Wilson and with Flush, she assures him that: "Your letters to me I take with me, let the 'ounces' cry out aloud, ever so. I *tried* to leave them, and I could not. That is, they would not be left: it was not my fault—I will not be scolded. Is this my last letter to you, ever dearest? [and it was] Oh—if I loved you less . . . a little, little less. . . . Do you pray for me to-night, Robert? Pray for me, and love me, that I may have the courage, feeling both—. Your own Ba." [79]

The words speak eloquently of her devotion and her love, but they speak vigorously also of her courage and her sensitivity. Elizabeth Barrett Browning, a person in her own right, has not deserved the lily-label, the hallmark of the languishing Victorian female. Few, given her health and familial circumstances, would have dared at twenty what she dared at forty; the feat was herculean. Perhaps closer attention to her letters would rid the critical world of the erroneous portrait sketched by the Besier play. She herself is as unlike that shadow-Ba portrayed therein as Athena is to Elsie Dinsmore.

The letters of Elizabeth Barrett Browning form, as we have seen, a treasure trove of her thoughts and ideas. From them we can learn more about her than we can from the vast horde of biographies. Rich as the letters are as a source for personal detail, they are equally rich as a source for her critical opinions; and a detailed study of them would form a book in and of itself. For our purposes, however, it is sufficient that they show her a compassionate, astute, intelligent, and wryly humorous critic whose qualities of mind and heart demonstrate that she deserves a higher rank as literary commentator than she has heretofore received.

Providing rich background for her excellent sonnet sequence, the letters to and about Robert Browning are, as we have seen, full of the pith and marrow of *being* requisite to fine poetry. But it is to that poetry itself that we must turn if we are to test the result.

CHAPTER 6

Parnassus Attained: Sonnets from the Portuguese

O N July 22, 1846, Elizabeth Barrett wrote to Robert Browning: "I did not go out yesterday, and was very glad not to have a command laid on me to go out, the wind blew so full of damp and dreariness. Then it was pleasanter to lie on the sofa and think of you, which I did, till at last I actually dreamed of you, falling asleep for that purpose." [1] During those times when the London weather was chill and clammy, when the wind wailed up and down Wimpole Street, she quite likely turned her thoughts inward and wrote those sonnets for which she still enjoys a measure of renown. The *Sonnets from the Portuguese,* written during the period of their courtship, drift thematically between reality and dream just as the poet drifts in her reverie between the harsh reality of London's inclement weather, so like her life as she knows it, and the pleasant, though seemingly impossible, dream of her love for Robert and of his for her. In this same letter she writes: "You shall see some day at Pisa what I will not show you now. Does not Solomon say that 'there is a time to read what is written.' If he doesn't, he *ought.*" [2] But Robert Browning was not to see the love sonnets even at Pisa.

I *A Gift of Love*

After the birth of Pen, the Brownings stayed at Bagni di Lucca. Reviewing the genesis of the sonnets in her splendid *Variorum Edition,* Fanny Ratchford quotes Elizabeth as saying to her husband: "Do you know I once wrote some poems about you? . . . There they are, if you care to see them." [3] We are told that Robert Browning thought them the "finest sonnets written in any language since Shakespeare's" [4] ; and, because of his persistence, the sonnets were published. Elizabeth thought them too personal to be published under her own name, and for that reason the two poets decided to disguise them as a translation. The title *Sonnets from the Portuguese* had a dual source: partly because Elizabeth was dark-complexioned, Browning often referred to her as "my little Portuguese"; also, her poem "Caterina to Camoëns" intrigued him. The Portuguese poet Camoëns had known a great love in the past, just as Robert and Elizabeth now knew it. Thus, disguise and sentiment were served by the quaint title.

Although Edmund Gosse insisted in *Critical Kit-Kats* that the sonnets were published privately in 1847, stating that the manuscript was sent to Elizabeth's friend Mary Russell Mitford, he was wrong.[5] His reference, the so-called Reading Edition of the sonnets, has been demonstrated to be an out-and-out forgery. The complete text of the sonnets, with the exception of Sonnet XLII, appeared in the revised edition of her *Poems* of 1844, published by Chapman and Hall in 1850. Subsequently, revisions of this same edition appeared in 1853 and 1856. Finally, in 1897, Frederic Kenyon, supposedly at the author's own suggestions, brought out the edition of the sonnets which he guaranteed to be "authentic."[6] The best modern edition of the sonnets is, of course, the *Variorum* (which is difficult to find); and it contains variants from three manuscripts: the ones located in the Library of the British Museum, in the Pierpont Morgan Library, and in the Houghton Library.

There are forty-four sonnets in the sequence in the *Variorum.* While no sonnet is dated, as Miss Ratchford indicates, the progression is logical and easy to see. With the availability of the *Love Letters,* it is relatively easy to connect this progression with the day-to-day life of the two poets during their courtship. The sonnets may be approached, of course, without attention to biography. They are highly personal expressions of love, as are many fifteenth- and sixteenth-century sonnet sequences; but their universality makes them appeal to almost every man and woman. They were not written as exercises to a patron, nor were they written for just any man by just any woman: they were written by a poet to a poet, and this factor very likely gives them their peculiar grace. To know something, therefore, of the joys and sorrows, of the peace and turmoil, in the lives of these poets during the year 1845–46 yields a measure of understanding which is lacking when a purely technical approach is invoked.

As an example of the value of using the *Love Letters* as one approach to an analysis and criticism of the sonnets, we may cite Alethea Hayter's otherwise excellent study of Mrs. Browning's poetic technique.[7] Miss Hayter's textual criticism of the *Sonnets from the Portuguese* causes certain problems for her as when she objects that they are "not enough removed from personal relationship to universal communication. They are hardly sensual at all, but emotionally they are naked—wonderful for the lover to whom they were addressed, but in some way uncomfortable for the rest of us." [8] Miss Hayter also asserts that the "much-praised 'Sonnets from the Portuguese' are not her [Elizabeth Barrett Browning's] best work because in them she is dealing with an emotion too new and powerful for her to transmute it into universally valid terms." [9] Moreover, she continues, Mrs. Browning's sonnets do not speak for all of us; for, unlike Shakespeare or Meredith in their sonnet sequences, Elizabeth's "sonnets express the love of one particular individual for another; they are personal, even idiosyncratic." [10] They *are* personal; but, as we have stated, they do speak the universal language of love while remaining peculiar to the being of Elizabeth Barrett Browning. The fact that she spent a great amount of time alone in her room at 50 Wimpole Street by no means made her a stranger to love. To make this point, however, the sonnets themselves must be permitted to speak.

II   *Analysis of the Sonnets*

The first of Elizabeth's *Sonnets from the Portuguese* announces the revitalization of her waning life through the efficacy of love. The biographical background is clear: the poet, nearing forty, ill and wasted, besieged by sadness and disappointment, has looked forward to and resigned herself to death, as countless letters from her to Robert Browning testify. In the opening sonnet, she muses how Theocritus had sung nostalgically of things past; and his song invokes in her that which she has had in life and also that which she has missed. What she has missed brings tears to her eyes, and she gently weeps; but, as she weeps for that which can not be, a masterful force moves behind her: "Straightway I was 'ware,/ So weeping, how a mystic Shape did move/ Behind me, and drew me backward by the hair,/ And a voice said in mastery while I strove, . . ./ 'Guess now who holds thee?' " [11] The poet answers the question with "Death," but the voice replies, "Not Death, but Love."

In nucleus, this sonnet expresses one of the strongest, most poignant strains in the sequence. Death has been the compelling force for years; for, because of her physical debilitation, her spirit has longed for release. But she must now change her attitude; she is forced to do so by the impulse, an overridingly strong one, to love and be loved. The shape of love is *mystic*: it transcends the what we know empirically to the what we know only intuitively. The masterful voice is one of love, not of death; and the term *silver* connotes value: "But, there,/ The silver answer rang ... 'Not Death, but Love.' " Nevertheless, there is violence in this sonnet: the masterful "mystic Shape" grabs her by the hair and violently wrenches her backward, and she struggles against it.

Such skillful use of imagery strikes us with consummate force, for only a violent action could wrench the poet from her tedious routine. Accustomed for five years to think of impending death, she must now learn to cope with an entirely different mode: love is for the living, and she must live. Many of the subsequent sonnets in the sequence treat this problem of how to cope with love, which demands an accent on living, and of how to refute and set aside the lassitude and apathy to which she had accustomed herself while waiting for death.

In Sonnet III (41), Browning's urgency is compared with her own acquiescence; for, as she states in the opening line, "Unlike are we, unlike, O princely Heart!," so much unlike are they that she has their two guardian angels look askance at each other, wondering how two such diverse spirits can ever enjoy compatability. She is aware that he is the vigorous, joyful, "Chief musician" and that he sings at court, "A guest for queens to social pageantries." She is "A poor, tired, wandering singer ... singing through/ The dark, and leaning up a cypress tree," a death image. He is crowned with light while on her the dew of death rests. The last line, "And Death must dig the level where these agree," suggests that, since their differences are too great to become reconciled in this life, death alone can find for them a common meeting place.

The imagery in Sonnet III is strikingly appropriate as a reflection of the essential differences in the two poets' modes of living. The opening line, "Unlike are we, unlike, O princely Heart!," announces the controlling thought of the sonnet; and, as we have seen, it remains consistent throughout the fourteen lines. Living for some five years like a mole in her chamber at Wimpole Street, Elizabeth recognizes the vitality and verve of Robert Browning's presence in the drawing rooms and coffee shops of London. He has been and is at home in society. She, on the other hand, enervated by illness and by the drugs she took to assuage her pain, has sought the solitude of her room, where she could be alone with thought and spirit—a quiet punctuated only by the brief appearances of her family, her maid, and the continual presence of her dog, Flush. In Sonnet III she comes closer to the truth than Romanticists care to admit: she was embarked on an impossible mission, and she had the intelligence to know it. Those who look upon Elizabeth as a "dreamer" would do well to consider the hard line of thought which her metaphors cloak. She was far more of a realist than her biographers have chosen to portray her.

Sonnet IV (43) develops the theme of Sonnet III, for in it she juxtaposes the sense of her own decay with Robert Browning's vital, "golden" voice. He is full of ideas, of energy, of song. He is "Most gracious singer of high poems!" Her "house's latch" is too poor for his vital hand, for she lives with "bats and owlets" nesting in her roof, but his song belongs only in a palace. Her voice is as the "cricket chirp" to his strong "mandolin." She weeps over the difference, but she acknowledges that he must sing "alone, aloof." The differences between the person and personality of Browning and her own, expressed in sonnets III and IV, weigh heavily upon her. The culmination comes in Sonnet V, one of the most successful of the sonnets because it is one of the most compressed and because its central image is a unifying one. The controlling image is a familiar one, the ashes from an "unextinguished hearth," as Shelley before her expressed these latent thoughts. Her heavy heart is likened to Electra's sepulchral urn:

> I lift my heavy heart up solemnly,
> As once Electra her sepulchral urn,
> And, looking in thine eyes, I overturn
> The ashes at thy feet. Behold and see
> What a great heap of grief lay hid in me,
> And how the red wild sparkles dimly burn
> Through the ashen greyness. If thy foot in scorn
> Could tread them out to darkness utterly,
> It might be well perhaps. But if instead
> Thou wait beside me for the winds to blow
> The grey dust up, . . . those laurels on thine head,
> O my beloved, will not shield thee so,
> That none of all the fires shall scorch and shred
> The hair beneath. Stand further off then! go.
>
> (45)

Miss Hayter states that this sonnet, fine though it is, is somewhat spoiled for her because Electra's urn did not contain the ashes or Orestes. "She only thought it did," writes Miss Hayter in her study of Elizabeth Barrett Browning.[12] For Elizabeth, however, thought holds the kind of reality that transcends the mundane. For her, thought often *is* reality. And in the *Sonnets from the Portuguese* hers is a fortunate, if oblique, point of view.

She undoubtedly knew all about Electra and the urn, and that Electra was being fooled, In a sense, Elizabeth's empathy could extend to and encompass the situation; for she was used to being an observer;

she was used to being passive and acted upon. The sensitivity which the sonnet reflects is the peculiar treasure of Elizabeth Barrett Browning. With the insight she has gained through her years of seclusion, she knows that she offers little but ashes to her lover. She is not sixteen, twenty, or even thirty: she is almost forty, she is ill; she has lost her beloved Bro; she has become alienated from her father; and she has the perspective that experience brings to an intelligent and wise person. Thus if Browning's foot treads any latent spark out, it may be for the best. For, should he wait patiently beside her and give the flame a chance to revitalize itself, he may be burned in consequence. Her spirit is willing, but her flesh is weak and failing; therefore, she admonishes him to go from her while there is yet time. The laurels on his head will not, she states, be sufficient to shield him from the weight which caring for her will impose on him. She sees herself as a potential burden to him, and this she does not wish to be.

Early in the first year of the courtship, Elizabeth poignantly alludes to the differences between them in a letter to Robert dated March 20, 1845:

And what you say of society draws me on to many comparative thoughts of your life and mine. You seem to have drunken of the cup of life full, with the sun shining on it. I have lived only inwardly; or with *sorrow*, for a strong emotion. . . . I grew up in the country—had no social opportunities, had my heart in books and poetry, and my experience in reveries. My sympathies drooped towards the ground like an untrained honeysuckle—and but for *one,* in my own house—but of this I cannot speak [an allusion to her beloved Bro]. It was a lonely life, growing green like the grass around it. Books and dreams were what I lived in—and domestic life only seemed to buzz gently around, like the bees about the grass.[13]

And, a little later, she writes to him that he will be disappointed when he meets her; for she has nothing to offer such a wonderfully alive man as he: "There is nothing to see in me; nor to hear in me—I never learnt to talk as you do in London; although I can admire that brightness of carved speech in Mr. Kenyon and others. If my poetry is worth anything to any eye, it is the flower of me. I have lived most and been most happy in it, and so it has all my colours; the rest of me is nothing but a root, fit for the ground and the dark."[14] These are but two of the many allusions she makes to their differences which show her realistic view of their situation.

In Sonnet VI (47), however, she sees that, while he may go from her, it is too late, in reality, for her to withdraw. She is caught up in the love; and, to her, they have become one, even though dire consequences may follow. When she prays to God for herself, she prays also for her lover; in her eyes are seen the tears for and of two. Psychologically, she recognizes the rift between head and heart: the first makes her realistic and results in sonnets devoted to the truth as others may see it; the second, however, involves her in a dialogue with her innermost being because she knows that she ought not feel as she does, but she cannot bring her reason to conquer her heart.

In Sonnet VII (49), we see her conviction that he has not only wrought change in her life, but that he has literally saved her from what she thought was her destiny, death; and the *Love Letters,* like the sonnet sequence, support and reaffirm consistently this point. Very telling are the lines in Sonnet VII: "I, who thought to sink,/ Was caught up into love, and taught the whole/ Of life in a new rhythm." Learning this "new rhythm" is not easy; indeed, the lessons can be traumatic, both physically and mentally. Moreover, when she wonders in Sonnet VIII (51) what she can give him, "What can I give thee back, O liberal/ And princely giver, who has brought the gold/ And purple of thine heart, unstained, untold,/ And laid them on the outside of the wall/ For such as I to take or leave withal"—she tells him that not coldness stops her from returning his love but that the colors of her life have been run into "pale stuff" by her tears and are fit only for his footsteps to tread upon.

In extending the imagery of clothes from his royal colors to her own vestments, pale and dim, she achieves again the central effect in contrasting his mode of living and himself with hers and herself, as she sees them. Sonnet IX (53) extends this comparison: his colors are still the royal purple she associates with him; but her *being* is dust that will sully his colors, and her essential self is poisonous to him. She does not regard the two of them as equals; for that reason, any gift she bestows on him will be ungenerous, even though it be her best, her love. But she cannot leave her situation in this state, nor does she; for, shocked out of her habitual mode of existence, she rallies in Sonnet X (55) to contrast what she *feels* with what she *is.* In Sonnet X, her love burns bright, like fire to match the purple and gold of his being and his love: "Fire is bright,/ Let temple burn, or flax. An equal light/ Leaps in the flame from cedar-plank or weed./ And love is fire." She turns this idea over and over in her mind. While she herself may be dim, her flame matches his, transfigured by his. She interjects that idea that the meanest of God's creatures, loving Him, is accepted by God through love.

Students often find Elizabeth confusing on the subject of God, Love, and Robert Browning. For her, however, no confusion exists: God is Love; and Robert Browning's love brought concrete form to the concept: in a Platonic sense, it gave form to the formless. The flame of love is divine in origin; it burns through lovers; its fire distills all lesser metal out; what remains is the pure essence. For that reason, Elizabeth feels equally at home, where love is concerned, with either God or Robert Browning. As she summarizes: "And what I *feel,* across the inferior features/ Of what I *am,* doth flash itself, and show/ How that great work of Love enhances Nature's." Sonnets XI, XII, and XIII play upon the same theme found in Sonnet X: she does have something equal to offer. Since she loves him, she is equal and bears a worthy gift: "Indeed this very love which is my boast,/ And which, when rising up from breast to brow,/ Doth crown me with a ruby large enow/ To draw men's eyes and prove the inner cost . . ." (59). Even so, the gift was his because she would not have had it had he not "shown me how." But he has shown her; and she is, therefore, more confident of being worthier of his love than the earlier expressions indicate.

In the well-known Sonnet XIV, she does not wish their love to be superficial or contrived: she does not want him to love her for her smile, her manner of speaking, or, for that matter, her manner of thinking. All of these things are, she suggests, subject to alteration and change. Perhaps Shakespeare's Sonnet 116 was in her mind; or, perhaps, the sonnet simply reflects the wish of lovers everywhere to transcend the mundane, the transitory, to attempt to love sublimely forever. For her, as for Shakespeare, "love is not love/ Which alters when it alteration findes,/ Or bends with the remover to remove./ O no, it is an ever fixed marke/ That looks on tempests and is never shaken." In order to assure this permanence, she implores her lover:

> If thou must love me, let it be for nought
> Except for love's sake only. Do not say
> "I love her for her smile . . . her look . . . her way
> Of speaking gently, . . . for a trick of thought
> That falls in well with mine, and certes brought
> A sense of pleasant ease on such a day—
> For these things in themselves, Beloved, may
> Be changed, or change for thee,—and love, so wrought,
> May be unwrought so. Neither love me for

Thine own dear Pity's wiping my cheeks dry,—
A creature might forget to weep, who bore
Thy comfort long, and lose thy love thereby!
But love me for love's sake, that evermore
Thou may'st love on, through love's eternity."

(63)

Sonnet XXI (77) also asks that, while he speak over and over of his love
for her, he not forget to love her in silence, or as she says, "with thy
soul." Understandably, the sonnets that mark their differences need a
balancing group which indicate the lovers' common bond. And that
bond, it becomes increasingly clear, is their love that wells up from the
soul.

In Sonnet XXII, the line: "When our two souls stand up erect and
strong" is as forceful and vigorous as their love. She asks what wrong
the world can do them when confronted with such spiritual vigor.
Paradoxically, she prefers to stay in the world rather than mount to
heaven; for the strength and unique quality of their love will preserve
their pure spirits from "Contrarious moods of men" and gain for them
"A place to stand and love in for a day" (79). Sonnet XXIII reiterates
her willingness to exchange heaven for earth because of him. While
some have given up "acres and degree" for their lovers, she has but one
thing to give up for him, death: "I yield the grave for thy sake, and
exchange/ My near sweet view of Heaven, for earth with thee!" (81). In
Sonnet XXIV she also notes the sharpness of the world, its ability to
cut into the softness of love; but she affirms that they can shut out the
"stab of worldlings" because they are guarded by the "charm" of love
(83).

The thought progression in the sonnets shows the growth of love,
the deepening into mature love when, come what may, the lovers
resolve to stand against the world, regardless of those "slings and arrows
of outrageous fortune" so indigenous to it. Wholeheartedly Elizabeth
has accepted the fact of viable love in her life and the dramatic change
which it has wrought. Of this change she speaks explicitly in at least
two sonnets. In Sonnet XXV she again refers to the "heavy heart" that
was hers before meeting Browning; and the imagery is heavy, the tone
dull. She refers to her attempt to lift her heart "Above the world
forlorn," but she finds that even the grace of God has difficulty in
helping her do so. Then Browning comes, she says, and bids her "drop
[her heart] adown [his] calmly great/ Deep being!" (85). There in the
depth of him her heart beats, "mediating/ Betwixt the stars and the

unaccomplished fate." The picture presented is that of a woman attempting to lift a heavy burden by herself and finally finding the solution: to drop it into the depth of another being where comfort, warmth, and help reside.

Another sonnet stressing the change his love has wrought in her life is Sonnet XXVI (87), in which she expresses the change from vicarious to direct living which he has effected in her. This sonnet is often cited as a reference to her isolation and solitary ways, and so it is; but we cannot accept it as literal truth, for we have seen how relatively full her life was. She is a poet; and, like Keats, she too has found those "realms of gold" highly satisfactory. Early in the *Love Letters* she has written to Browning regarding her world of books and the poetic pleasures derived therefrom, saying: "Like to write? Of course, of course I do. I seem to live while I write—it is life, for me. Why, what is to live? Not to eat and drink and breathe,—but to feel the life in you down all the fibres of being, passionately and joyfully." [15]

The pleasures of the vicarious, however, are constantly honed by contact with the real world. When she was well enough to venture into society—to meet with Kenyon, Wordsworth, and Miss Mitford—she could return to the world of books all the more prepared to test the vicarious against the actual. The first lines of Sonnet XXVI attest to this life of the mind:

> I lived with visions for my company,
> Instead of men and women, years ago,
> And found them gentle mates, nor thought
> A sweeter music than they played to me.

Until she saw that these visions became dusty and silent as the world with its cares, sorrows, and blight grew more and more urgently apparent, even though she retreated further and further from it. Reality reappears to her in the form of her lover, who now becomes what her visions once seemed. Her final line again reiterates that Browning is God's gift to her, and no dream can compare with it. He has (Sonnet XXVII) lifted her from the "drear flat of earth" and breathed life into her almost as God breathed life into dust. She who had looked only for God, found her ideal in her lover: "And I who looked for only God, found *thee!*" (89). While her father had fallen short of her ideal, Robert Browning had met it. [16]

With one exception, the sonnets from XXIII to the last, XLIV, are affirmative and lack any expression of regret. The exception, Sonnet

XXXV, quite naturally questions whether or not she will regret forsaking home and family for Robert. At forty, having lived literally in the midst of home and family, we cannot wonder at the thought, for it is a realistic doubt:

> If I leave all for thee, wilt thou exchange
> And be all to me? Shall I never miss
> Home-talk and blessing and the common kiss
> That comes to each in turn. . . .
>
> (105)

Even her sorrowful memories are, she knows, likely to be overshadowed by this new and vital love. Here she refers to Bro's dead but loving eyes, which for her can never change; for he is a part of the beloved past. She states that, because she has grieved for so long, she is "hard to love." Yet she resolves all by asking her lover to love her: "Open thine heart wide,/ And fold within, the wet wings of thy dove." In Sonnet XXXVII (109) she begs pardon of her lover that she has vacillated so within the sonnet sequence. She knows his strength to be that of the Divine, and she apologizes for making his image in sand, saying that the years of her life without him were reluctant to take his "sovranty" and "Have forded my swimming brain to undergo/ Their doubt and dread, and blindly to forsake/ Thy purity of likeness, and distort/ Thy worthiest love to a worthless counterfeit." She has returned to the theme that this love is too good to be true or feasible.

Sonnet XLIII (121) deserves careful study on many counts. First of all, it is the culminating expression of her love. Second, it is widely adored by some and just as widely reviled by others. The sonnet is very likely as controversial as Joyce Kilmer's "Trees"—but, a much better poem, it is undeserving of the condemnation it has received. To look at two points of view regarding fairly recent criticism of this sonnet is interesting, although not particularly informative. Robert B. Heilman finds the sonnet full of abstract imagery, glaring generalizations, and reminiscences of platform rhetoric.[17] William Going, in an answer to Professor Heilman's criticism, demonstrates that Elizabeth summarizes in Sonnet XLIII eight ways of loving, each of which she has previously considered in a preceding sonnet. Thus, he argues, she has every right to generalize in Sonnet XLIII because it is a conclusive sonnet.[18]

We agree with Professor Going's justification of the imagery, but there is another and perhaps more accurate way to look at Sonnet XLIII. The sonnet is Platonic in orientation; we need to consider the following passage from the *Symposium.*

He who has been instructed thus far in the things of love, and who has learned to see the beautiful in due order and succession, when he comes toward the end will suddenly perceive a nature of wondrous beauty . . . a nature which in the first place is everlasting, not growing and decaying, or waxing and waning; secondly, not fair in one point of view and foul in another, or at one time or in one relation or at one place fair, at another time or in another relation or at another place foul . . . but beauty absolute, separate, simple, and everlasting, which without diminution and without increase, or any change, is imparted to the ever-growing and perishing beauties of all other things. He who from these ascending under the influence of true love, begins to perceive that beauty, is not far from the end. And the true order of going, or being led by another, to the things of love, is to begin from the beauties of earth and mount upwards for the sake of that other beauty, using these as steps only, and from one going on to two, and from two to all fair forms, and from fair forms to fair practices, and from fair practices to fair notions, until from fair notions he arrives at the notion of absolute beauty, and at last knows what the essence of beauty is.[19]

This passage is pertinent because, throughout the *Sonnets from the Portuguese,* we have seen Elizabeth struggle to give expression to her love. She has compared and contrasted herself with her lover; she has vacillated between doubt that she is worthy and confidence that love ennobles all; she has selected the imagery of birds and royal clothes, of religion, of God, of marble statuary, of flowers, urns, tears, and hearts—symbols of freedom, honor, and central permanence. On the other hand, she has referred to the practice of exchanging locks of hair (XVIII, XIX), to his calling her by her pet name (XXXIII), and to her daily letters received from him that mark the stages of romantic progression (XXVIII). She has moved, in short, from the weighty to the trivial, and back again from the light to the profound. She has told him how she once sought beauty and reality in books, then in nature, but now in love she sees what transfigures all. She has moved up the ladder of abstraction from fair forms, instructed by love, to that absolute beauty concomitant with ideal love.

Proof of this movement lies in an astonishingly explicit prose parallel in one of her love letters to Browning. She writes that she has loved him all her life, "unawares, that is, the idea of you."[20] She admits that it is habitual for women to love an ideal, to search for it for years, and, finally, to compromise. But, in words strikingly close to those of Sonnet LXIII, she declares that she has not needed to compromise since he is a perfect copy of the ideal: "One's ideal must be above one, as a matter of course, you know. It is as far as one can reach with one's eyes (soul-eyes), not reach to touch. And here is mine . . . shall I tell you? . . . even to the visible outward sign of the black hair and the complexion (why you might ask my sisters!)." [21] And, in conclusion, she supports the point made here that his love, to her, is on a level with that of God: "Right or wrong it may be, but true it *is,* and I tell you. Your love has been to me like God's own love, which makes the receivers of it kneelers." [22]

Looking carefully at Sonnet XLIII, we can see her entire experience recapitulated as she attempts to answer the question all true lovers at some time pose to one another: "How do I love thee?" She begins to count the ways: "I love thee to the depth and breadth and height/ My soul can reach, when feeling out of sight/ For the ends of Being and ideal Grace." Quite obviously, she had chosen to express the "nth" degree of love: her consummate grasp of the absolute. Necessarily, she must use abstract terms; for the concept itself requires them. Thus "ends of Being and ideal Grace" are appropriate terms here. Taken in conjunction with the lines that follow, "I love thee to the level of everyday's/ Most quiet need, by sun and candlelight," we see her juxtapose the abstract with the concrete. To return to the quotation from the *Symposium,* we can readily see that she has indeed "learned to see the beautiful in due order and succession"; and, in her opening line, she has come to "perceive a nature of wondrous beauty. . . ." This perception sends her to the abstract for expression of her grasp.

When she states in the next lines "I love thee freely, as men strive for Right;/ I love thee purely, as they turn from Praise," she is again in accord with the concept of ideal love as explicated in the *Symposium.* In these lines she refers to "fair practices," which are part of true love. Following these lines, she invokes her total emotional commitment, both past and present, and gives it to her lover:

> I love thee with the passion put to use
> In my old griefs, and with my childhood's faith.
> I love thee with a love I seemed to lose
> With my lost saints,—I love thee with the breath,
> Smiles, tears, of all my life!—
>
> (p. 121)

Finally, she turns from this world to the next, saying, "and, if God choose,/ I shall but love thee better after death." Taking the things that belong to the everyday world, those of "most quiet need," the emotional experiences that she has had and that square with reality as all of us know it, she turns to a consideration of the permanence of true love. She realizes that this permanence is, ultimately, in the hands of God; but she herself has gone as far as any human being can go in this sonnet to commit herself to love Robert Browning.

III   *Related Letters*

The *Sonnets from the Portuguese* leave us an astonishingly clear record of the mind and heart of Elizabeth Barrett-Barrett. We are permitted to follow her incredulous surprise that Robert Browning could love her in spite of her very real resistance to his pleas through to her final and utter capitulation. Hers was no sentimental Victorian journey, for her problems were very real, and she was cruelly realistic in her self-analysis. In a revealing letter written to Miss Mitford on Friday, September 18, 1846, just after her marriage to Robert Browning in Marylebone Church, she pleads for understanding, saying: "I tell you solemnly that nothing your thoughts can suggest against this act of mine, has been unsuggested by *me* to *him.*" [23] She reveals that she had suspected Browning's suit to be "a mere poet's fancy . . . an illusion of a confusion between the woman and the poetry." [24] In a poignant passage, she explains to Miss Mitford how Browning has overcome her objections; but she cannot pinpoint the paramount reason why he should have been able to do so.

But ultimately she does delineate these reasons. The ideal of love, as expressed in Plato's dialogues, has ever been before her. [25] She tells Miss Mitford that marriage has never been to her the prime *desideratum,* that she has resisted the admonition of her friends to take "Mr. A or B or C for the 'best possible' whatever might be." [26] She asserts that she never could marry "a common man," for she has found such men lacking what she needed. She has, however, held fast to the ideal of love, believing only that a man who incorporated all in all, and whom she could love, could never love her.

It is obvious from the following, as it is from the sonnets, that she found her ideal; for, in speaking of Browning, she writes: "Whether it was that an unusual alikeness of mind or (the high and the low may be alike in the general features) . . . a singular closeness of sympathy on a thousand subjects . . . drew him fast to me—or whether it was *love simple* . . . which after all is *love proper* . . . an unreasonable instinct, accident . . . 'falling,' as the idiom says . . . the truth became obvious that he would be happier with me than apart from me—and I . . . why I

am only as any other woman in the world, with a heart belonging to
her." [27] But that she was not *any* woman in the world has been
demonstrated by the skill with which she revealed her turbulent
thoughts in these forty-four sonnets. To Robert himself, she writes
truthfully:

It is true of me—very true—that I have not a high appreciation of what
passes in the world . . . under the name of love; and that a distrust of
the thing had grown to be a habit of mind with me when I knew you
first. It has appeared to me, through all the seclusion of my life and the
narrow experience it admitted of, that in nothing men—and women
too—were so apt to mistake their own feelings, as in this one thing.
Putting falseness quite on one side, quite out of sight and consideration,
an honest mistaking of feeling appears wonderfully common, and no
mistake has such frightful results—none can. [28]

Elizabeth Barrett harkens back in this letter to Plato's concept of the
"noble error," but she looks ahead realistically to that which she herself
has seen in her own contemporary society. She then speaks of
overhearing a conversation between her brother and one of his married
friends in which the friend remarks of his own wife, that he had
"ruined his prospects by marrying." The way things ought to be and
the way things often are, that is, the ideal compared with the
supposedly real, gave Elizabeth not only pause for thought but also
cause for delay. Again she is truthful with Robert Browning, for in the
same letter she offers the following explanation for her reluctance to
succumb to his entreaties:

People used to say to me, "You expect too much—you are too
romantic." And my answer always was that "I could not expect too
much when I expected nothing at all" . . . which was the truth—for I
never thought (and how often I have *said that*!) I never thought that
anyone whom I could love, would stoop to love *me* . . . the two things
seemed clearly incompatible, to my understanding.
    And now when it comes in a miracle, you wonder at me for looking
twice, thrice, four times, to see if it comes through ivory or *horn*. You
wonder that it should seem to me at first all illusion—illusion for
you,—illusion for me as a consequence. But how natural. [29]

We cannot but admire her intelligence, her truthfulness, her humility,
and her very real awareness that the world as she had found it was
excitingly changing for her into a private world which she had dreamed
might someday come to pass. She has given up on the notion that it

would, but the hope remained deeply buried in her quintessential self that it might.

As for the technical aspects of the *Sonnets from the Portuguese,* Miss Hayter's work is indispensable.[30] The Petrarchan form, consisting of two quatrains and a sestet—more familiarly described in the octave-sestet terms—was well known to Elizabeth. The turn comes at the end of the octave and the beginning of the sestet, allowing the poet to enlarge upon her subject or take an altered direction. In developing a Petrarchan sonnet, the poet usually announces his subject in the first four lines; develops it in the next four; and then, having executed the new direction, attempts to resolve the conflict or ease the emotional strain in the sestet.[31] As Miss Hayter indicates, Elizabeth Barrett Browning does not often shift and put the turn in the proper place.[32] she often runs into the sestet before she offers a solution, as in Sonnet VII; but this is not a serious fault when we consider the impact of most of her conclusive lines in which she displays a considerable amount of dramatic power and compression.

Miss Hayter also argues against Elizabeth's use of the "tone of speech"[33] in many of the sonnets. We can, indeed, hear her talking across the ages to her lover: but can we not also hear Shakespeare talking through the ages to his beloved in the following and in numerous other sonnets to Mr. W. H.?

> O thou my lovely Boy who in thy power,
> Doest hould times fickle glasse, his sickle, hower;
> Who has by wayning grouwne, and therein shou'st,
> Thy lovers withering as thy sweet selfe grow'st.
>
> (Sonnet 126)

If there is a more relaxed and intimate approach suggested in Elizabeth's sonnets than in those of Shakespeare, we must remember that she is not only centuries in time after Shakespeare, but she also prided herself on being *au courant* in the techniques and poetry could use. She was not hidebound to tradition, and she would not permit herself to be; for she rejected the idea that a poet should listen only to the voices of the past. In a revealing excerpt from a letter to Robert Browning, she comments on the value of the past versus that of the present in relation to art forms and innovations:

I am inclined to think that we want new *forms,* as well as thoughts. The old gods are dethroned. Why should we go back to the antique moulds, classical moulds, as they are so improperly called? If it is a necessity of

Art to do so, why then those critics are right who hold that Art is exhausted and the world too worn out for poetry. I do not, for my part, believe this: and I believe the so-called necessity of Art to be the mere feebleness of the artist. Let us all aspire rather to *Life,* and let the dead bury their dead. If we have but courage to face these conventions, to touch this low ground, we shall take strength from it instead of losing it; and of that, I am intimately persuaded. For there is poetry *everywhere;* the "treasure" . . . lies all over the field.[34]

If the *Sonnets from the Portuguese* put old thoughts into new forms, they do what Elizabeth intended; that is, her heady, though Platonic, old wine went into new bottles, the variation on the Petrarchan sonnet form. It is very likely that with her background in poetic form she not only knew what she was doing, but she also condoned her technique from a philosophical point of view.

Finally, the *Sonnets from the Portuguese* have a distinct ring of truth. The thoughts they express are no empty conventional exercises but, rather, are manifestations of the profound love Elizabeth Barrett knew for Robert Browning. Her powerful lyric voice ringing out the truth of her love makes these sonnets stand as her most valuable contribution to the poetry of the world.

CHAPTER 7

Politics and Poets

IN spite of the accolades bestowed upon the political poems of the 1850's by our contemporary critics, the poems themselves are apt to strike a twentieth-century reader as dull. We do not, for example, have the interest in the battle for Italian unification that Mrs. Browning had. For her it was a passionate *cause célèbre* which consumed her thought and sapped her vitality far beyond the point it should have in view of her waning physical strength; for her interest in Italian politics was daily, and it was consummate. From her windows at Casa Guidi she observed and recorded, in that third person so characteristic of her prefaces, her "personal impressions, whose only value is in the intensity with which they were received, as proving her warm affection for a beautiful and unfortunate country, and the sincerity with which they are related, as indicating her own good faith and freedom from partisanship." [1]

I Casa Guidi Windows

Part I of *Casa Guidi Windows*[2] was written in 1847–48; Part II, in 1851. The second part is quite different from the first because of the fluctuations of fortune for the Italians; but the two taken together constitute Elizabeth's best political poem. Her editors, Porter and Clarke, call it "a condensed lyrical epic of a modern nation's birth"[3] and so, in some respects, it is. No one can fault the lilting lyricism of the opening lines:

> I heard last night a little child go singing
> > 'Neath Casa Guidi windows, by the church,
> O bella liberta, O bella!—stringing
> > The same words still on notes he went in search
> So high for. . . .
> > > > (ll. 1–5)

Nor can anyone doubt the sensitivity and profundity of Mrs. Browning's love affair with *bella Italia* when she writes of her own sense of unworthiness when confronted with that teeming womb of poets, Italy, graced by the golden Arno as it flows beneath the bridges of Florence: "Bent bridges, seeming to strain off like bows,/ And tremble while the arrowy undertide/ Shoots on and cleaves the marble as it goes,/ And strikes up palace-walls on either side,/ And froths the cornice out in glittering rows..." (ll. 55–59). This exquisitely beautiful imagery, significant of the glory of Italy, is juxtaposed with equally effective—though horrible—allusions to the poison and decay experienced by those who fight against the establishment:

> . . . Michel's Night and
>   Day
> And Dawn and Twilight wait in marble scorn
>   Like dogs upon a dunghill, couched on clay
> From whence the Medicean stamp's outworn,
>   The final putting off of all such sway
> By all such hands, and freeing of the unborn
>   In Florence and the great world outside Florence.
>   (ll. 73–79)

From *Casa Guidi Windows,* perhaps more than anywhere, her talent shines pure in its distillation. In this poetry, more than anywhere, she emulates the technique of Robert Browning as she weaves each seemingly trivial detail into a masterly tapestry of meaning. She returns to the little child who sings of a free Italy, a portent of the future. Having seen Elizabeth's struggles to express herself, we are astonished at the purity of her verse:

> Amen, great Angelo! the day's at hand.
> If many laugh not on it, shall we weep?
>   Much more we must not, let us understand.
> Through rhymers sonneteering in their sleep,
>   And archaists mumbling dry bones up the land,
> And sketchers lauding ruined towns a-heap,—
>   Through all that drowsy hum of voices smooth,
> The hopeful bird mounts carolling from the brake,
>   The hopeful child, with leaps to catch his growth,
> Sings open-eyed for liberty's sweet sake.
>   (ll. 145–54)

But, in spite of the marvelous poetry (and there is much of it that deserves the adjective), we cannot totally empathize with her devotion to the cause of Italian independence. Perhaps as there are more Hungarys, more Czechoslovakias, we shall find *Casa Guidi Windows* increasingly timely. Today, however, the poem is well-nigh forgotten except for scholars of the Victorian period and laid in a tomb, as is topical poetry everywhere. Certainly the struggle of the independent spirit to achieve a better life for all is admirable and, as such, fit subject for poetry; this independent spirit the poet chose to elevate in her political poems. She held no brief for any one form of government; for, as Miss Hayter points out, she was essentially a republican, but she believed in the right of the people to choose the form of government that best suited them.[4] Had she lived today, there is no doubt that her comments about our own world situation would make interesting reading; for, while she revered the independent spirit, she could never condone the violence often attendant upon its expression.[5]

II   *"Poems before Congress"*

In 1849, Elizabeth witnessed much from Casa Guidi's windows; and she wrote what she felt about it. In 1860, she issued another series of political poems, "Poems before Congress," [6] to which she wrote a very significant preface. Brief, concise, and effective, it raises the same issues which confront us today. In it she states that she wishes all men to rise above narrow patriotism in order to embrace the larger patriotic context of mankind, that is, loyalty to God. Her comment on nonintervention is as timely now as it was then: "non-intervention does not mean, passing by on the other side when your neighbour falls among thieves." [7] She looks for the day when an English statesman will see that the near-good for England is not necessarily the greater good for the world. Not only will this statesman see, he will also speak his message in clarion tones. Therefore she is timely for us, for certainly today we need the statesmen of the universe even more urgently than did England in the nineteenth century.

The controlling idea which prompted "Poems before Congress" was solid; its execution may well have been less substantial. The first poem, "Napoleon III in Italy," lauds Napoleon for his coup d'état. Needless to say, there were many who looked upon it as the beginning of days of infamy; but Elizabeth was not among these: to her, Napoleon III did what was necessary for the people, and that was what counted. Later in the poem, where she lauds him for coming to the aid of the Italians against the Austrians, she calls him "Sublime Deliverer!" (l. 94). Her exaggerated estimate was somewhat tempered later on, as we shall see, by the terms of the Peace of Villafranca; but at this time she instills a spirited quality in her verse as she describes the renewed vigor of the marching troops. Drawing upon incidents which had taken place in the various battles, she describes them with vigor and occasionally with pathos; and she concludes the poem with a last laurel bestowed upon Napoleon: "He came to deliver Italy. Emperor Evermore" (l. 416).

The poem is lusty and gusty, but those of us with some historical perspective may well wonder at the almost total lionization of Louis Napoleon; for, where her heroes were concerned, Elizabeth was generally aware of their faults as well as their virtues. For example, she admired Byron for his lyric quality; but she knew he lacked high seriousness. In the case of Napoleon III, she was aware of his shortcomings and indeed had alluded to them when he had first appeared on the historic scene. As time went on, however, her passion for Italy clouded her judgment somewhat; and anyone who seemed to help Italy, as Napoleon did seem to do at first, was revered by her. Napoleon had done much that was commendable: he had beautified Paris, legalized trade unions, and instituted various education reforms;[8] but it was not for these accomplishments that EBB sang his praises. It was because he chose to stand for Italy against Austria.

After the Peace of Villafranca, however, there were many who regarded him as one who had betrayed Italy. At the Treaty of Villafranca Napoleon agreed with Emperor Franz Joseph of Austria that Lombardy should be split from Venice and that Venice would be allied with Austria. No one in Italy was pleased, least of all Elizabeth. Mrs. Browning, in her poem on that subject, "A Tale of Villafranca," does not attack Napoleon for whatever part he must have played in this sad affair; rather, she puts the onus squarely on contentious statesmen. She says that no one could have worked with them, for they clouded every issue.

The tone of this poem is heavily satirical and trenchant. Her disappointment shows through bleakly as she addresses her little Florentine (her son, Pen) as follows:

> Ah child! ah child! I cannot say
> A word more. You conceive
> The reason now, why just to-day
> We see our Florence grieve.

> Ah child, look up into the sky!
> In this low world, where great Deeds die,
> What matter if we live?
>
> (ll. 77–84)

This bitter tone is repeated in another poem concerning the settlement with Franz Joseph. In "An August Voice" she makes Napoleon, the spokesman in the poem, state sardonically, "You'll take back your Grand-duke?/ I made the treaty upon it" (ll. 1–2), lines which refer to the reestablishment of those Italian dukes who had rushed away from their duchies and congregated at Gaeta at the first sign of trouble. The Florentines asked Grand Duke Leopold to return in an attempt to avoid Austrian occupation, but they were not happier with him as a man and as a ruler.

The dukes were not the only ones who fled to Gaeta to save their necks: Pius IX did also. In her poem "Christmas Gifts," Elizabeth delivers a volley in his direction. Once this Pope had been considered a liberal and was beloved by the people of Italy. From his seat in Gaeta, however, he issued an appeal to all Catholic powers to restore him to his throne in Rome; and Austria was, of course, a Catholic power. For this apparent betrayal of Italy, the Pope's popularity declined mightily; in fact, when he was finally restored to Rome, his policies became arbitrary and authoritarian,[9] thereby alienating him still more from his subjects. In addressing herself to the subject of the Pope's flight, Elizabeth lets the people ask, "who will show us where/ Is the stable where Christ was born?" (ll. 5–6). The Pope sits amid pomp and circumstance, surrounded by his cardinals, and asks for gold to barter for Italian duchies. A king of the West, however, offers him red, green, and white colors, the colors of Italy. With patriotism and devotion to Italy, the people will again see that Star in the East which will lead them to Christ. With this promise Elizabeth concludes a poem as memorable for its mediocrity as any she produced.

Two other poems of "Poems before Congress" take a different tack from these bitterly vitriolic works. "The Dance" involves an incident in which Italian ladies of the nobility invite the French officers who have come to the assistance of Italy to dance with them. The officers willingly oblige, and not a dry eye can be seen among the entire assemblage of patriotic Italians. Here, as always, Elizabeth portrays the French officers as saviors of Italy; and the tone of the poem is sentimental as an old song from our own antebellum days. While the diction is restrained and the action courteous, a great deal of emotional tension underlies the dignified statement. "A Court Lady" presents a vignette of a gracious, beautiful Italian lady—the symbol of Italian unification—who moves among the wounded from Lombardi, Tuscany, Venice, and Piedmont. The lady has robed herself in the most regal robes she has; and, as she moves among the wounded and dying the the military hospital, she calls them all "brothers," as befits her mission. The poem is marred by the typically strident sentimentality so characteristic of war poems of this era.

Both these poems, "The Dance" and "A Court Lady," are superficial when compared with the larger dimensions of "Italy and the World" a long, appreciative ode to the beauties and charms of Italy. It is, in addition, a denunciation of those Christian nations that have used her for their pleasure and profit but have not helped her when she was in need.

All of these poems treat of the complex problems which unification of Italy presented. The intricacies rise above the limits of this study, but the student who wishes to know more about it should consult the still excellent, though brief, *A Short History of the Italian People* by the distinguished Janet Trevelyan, from which most of the preceding background material has been drawn.

III   *Later Political Poems*

One poem which is also political or "sociological" remains to be discussed—"A Curse for a Nation." In its stretch beyond Italian politics, it embraces the universal problem of bondage and slavery. While it is directed at abuses of this kind everywhere, the poet very likely had America in mind; But her own countrymen took umbrage at the poem. In it, the poet is addressed by an angel who asks her to write "a curse for a nation." She protests that women should not curse, for they are too soft and sensitive for such a role. The angel is adamant, however, saying that there are women who curse and that the poet's obligation is to assume a similar role.

The poem is in two sections: the dialogue with the angel forms Part I; the curse itself, Part II. In the curse, the poet castigates a nation which pays lip service to freedom while keeping its foot calmly on bond-slaves. In such a nation, martyrs are strangled, despite the material prosperity which the nation enjoys. In the ten stanzas in which the curse is spun out we can readily see why the theme of the poem did not endear it to those countries, England and America, who believed themselves under attack. In this poem, as in political poems of all time, the writer risked her popularity; for she embraced unpopular causes. If the world looked askance at the rebellions in Italy, Elizabeth did not; If the world believed children and women should work long hours to bolster the economy; she did not agree; if the world justified slavery, she did not. She was not seeking popularity, she was seeking justice through truth. Wrong-headed as she sometimes was, her motives were above reproach.

As much as we might like to participate in her enthusiasm for Italian politics and thus enter into the spirit of her political poems, we are handicapped by time, distance, and the topicality of so many of them. Perhaps for this reason, most students of English literature who still read the poetry of Elizabeth Barrett Browning wish she had concentrated her powers upon the writing of sonnets and short lyrics. She was not to do so, however, except in very minor ways; for a list of the political poems in the last volume of her collected works illustrates that she is still absorbed in Italy. "First News from Villafranca" [10] again refers to the terms of the treaty. The gist of the poem is that the peace won at Villafranca is no peace at all, rather it is the calm interval " 'Twixt the tiger's spring and the crunch of the tooth" (l. 40). "King Victor Emanuel Entering Florence, April 1860" [11] praises another of her heroes, who did indeed eventually lead a united Italy. "Garibaldi" [12] praises the hero of Italy whom she had the satisfaction of seeing make inroads in Sicily before she died. "Mother and Poet" [13] is based on the actual life of Laura Savio of Turin, a poet in her own right, who lost two sons in battle within one year of each other in the Italian fracas.

IV *"De Profundis"*

It is with something of relief that we turn to the poetry that does not treat of the struggles to unify Italy, but there are few such poems; it is among the last ones published. One fine poem, "De Profundis," [14] was composed much earlier, probably in the years after Bro's death by drowning at Torquay (1840). Because the death of this brother had such a devastating effect on her, she very likely could not bear to publish the poem before 1860. The elegiac tone of the poem is intensified by the repetitive refrain at the end of each stanza: "my days go on." A sense of deep loss that pervades the work rises in a crescendo of grief in the following stanza, in which the poet cries at Nature's door, seeking some explanation of her loss:

> I knock and cry,—Undone, undone!
> Is there no help, no comfort,—none?
> No gleaning in the wide wheat plains
> Where others drive their loaded wains?
> My vacant days go on, go on.
>
> (ll. 36—40)

Finding no explanation forthcoming, she seeks for death to release her from earthly sorrow and to unite her with heavenly love, one manifested on earth formerly by the love she held for the now departed. She asks:

> Only to lift the turf unmown
> From off the earth where it has grown,
> Some cubit-space, and say "Behold,
> Creep in, poor Heart, beneath that fold,
> Forgetting how the days go on."
>
> (ll. 56—60)

Such is not to be, however, for God's voice answers her, not Nature's, as she had expected; and she knows that, as God is eternal, so is His plan for all the just and good. A partial reconciliation of the elegist takes place when she says:

> Whatever's lost, it first was won;
> We will not struggle nor impugn,
> Perhaps the cup was broken here,
> That heaven's new wine might show more clear.
> I praise thee while my days go on.
>
> (ll. 106—10)

The dignified and stately, powerful, expression of her grief is sustained consistently throughout the full one hundred and twenty lines of the poem. No faults common to her poetry show up here. The poem is a well-wrought unity and illustrative of the excellence she could achieve when she put her entire mind and being to the task.

V *"Lord Walter's Wife"*

The two poems "Lord Walter's Wife"[15] and "Bianca Among the Nightingales"[16] differ greatly in quality. The first is a strange and incoherent tale of Lord Walter's wife, who is speaking with a man we presume to be (or one who had formerly wished to be) her lover. At the opening of the poem, he is telling her that he will no longer stay near her because he fears her and believes she will strangle his soul in a mesh of her golden hair. She counters each of his reasons for choosing to leave her with a flippant answer. For example, when he says she has a young daughter who might be corrupted by the sight of her mother is participating in an illicit love tryst with him, she answers:

> "Oh, that," she said, "is no reason. The angels
>   keep out of the way;
> And Dora, the child, observes nothing, although you
>   should please me and stay."
>
> (ll. 17—18)

Incensed and outraged by her flippancy, he states that he has misjudged her badly; he could not possibly love such a shallow creature as she now seems to be. Whereupon she turns on him, with eyes blazing, to tell him she has ever been pure, fair, and innocent, while he himself, like many men, has attempted to seduce her. We learn that she loves Lord Walter and has always loved him, but has encouraged the other to prove to him that he did not really want her but was merely infatuated. At the end of the poem, she asks her daughter to help in inviting him to dinner; and we learn that he is a friend of Lord Walter's.

The poem is a failure. There is not scope enough in it to shift the characterization so rapidly. We cannot believe in either of the characters; they are one-dimensional and are never fully developed but disintegrate rapidly after the first twenty lines. Some of the dialogue is clever, but it is not convincing.

VI *"Bianca Among the Nightingales"*

"Bianca Among the Nightingales" is another matter. The opening stanza testifies that Elizabeth could still invoke considerable poetic power to produce effective imaginery, smooth rhyming, and clean, clear diction:

> The cypress stood up like a church
>   That night we felt our love would hold,
> and saintly moonlight seemed to search
>   And wash the whole world clean as gold;

> The olives crystallised the vales'
>   Broad slopes until the hills grew strong:
> The fire—flies and the nightingales
>   Throbbed each to either, flame and song.
> The nightingales, the nightingales!
>
>   (ll. 1—9)

In many ways, this poem is the most finished ballad she ever wrote. The story is one of a broken vow of love, and Bianca tells it. Her lover, Giulio, and she have vowed eternal love midst cypresses and moonlight while the nightingales sing. The scene here is Italy, but in Stanza IV the scene shifts to the cold moonlight of England and to an equally cold Englishwoman, to whom Giulio has succumbed, thereby breaking his vow to Bianca. Throughout Bianca's lament, the nightingales continue to sing, but their song is now a stabbing reminder of his betrayal. As she pictures Giulio flattering the Englishwoman, she hopes he will not barter his soul, which he has pledged to her; for each soul is to have, she says, but one love: "Yet souls are damned and love's profaned." And at this thought she cries: "These nightingales will sing me mad! The nightingales, the nightingales." (11.53-54) Bianca is obsessed with these birds that sing in her beloved Florence. "Betwixt our Tuscan trees that spring / As vital flames into the blue," and who also sing in the fogbound chill of London, midst "dull round blots of foliagement, / Like saturated sponges here / To suck the fogs up" (11.59-60). The poem is full of such striking contrasts.

Another effective contrast is that which the poet draws between the characters of Bianca and the Englishwoman. Bianca would have preferred to be poisoned, or to have had her eyes pricked out, than to have had her lover taken from her; for Bianca is fiery, impassioned, possessed of that warm Latin temperament associated with Italy. The Englishwoman, on the other hand, is "A worthless woman; mere cold clay," though exceedingly fair. Throughout the description, the nightingales sing on, but their song turns from melodic sweetness to grating harshness. Bianca's song ends bitterly with the following words:

> . . . . They sing for spite,
> They sing for hate, they sing for doom,
> They'll sing through death who sing through night,
> They'll sing and stun me in the tomb—
> The nightingales, the nightingales!
>
>   (ll. 140—44)

The ballad has more to it than many others we have seen before. The dramatic qualities are closer to those of a dramatic monologue, except that we have no listener as we do in the tonally similar poem, "Porphyria's Lover," by Robert Browning. There is, of course, the well-known and often ridiculed line, intended to be descriptive of the beauty of the Englishwoman: "What a head, / What leaping eyeballs." (1. 79). But this is really the sole defective image in the poem, though, granted, it is a glaring one! Other than this defect, the melodic and sensual lyricism of the opening stanzas when Bianca sings along with the nightingales of her true love and the increasing harshness of her song when she tells of Giulio's betrayal suffice to make this dramatic and passionate lyric one of the poet's best.

VII *"Where's Agnes?"*

Among the last poems to be published is the bitter "Where's Agnes?,"[17] which was written about a former friend of the poet who she believed to be a hypocrite (identified by Robert Browning as Mrs. Eckley whom the Brownings had often received in their home). The caustic, trenchant lines of the poem express Mrs. Browning's powerful aversion to what she considered a breach of faith.[18] The poem "My Kate"[19] portrays the antithesis of Agnes; for Kate, a sweet and pure soul, her inner qualities as profoundly true as Agnes' are profoundly putrid.

VIII *"A Musical Instrument"*

Included also in this final volume is the popular poem "A Musical Instrument,"[20] whose materials were drawn by the poet from the myth of Pan and Syrinx in Ovid's *Metamorphoses*. The poem is as forcefully lyrical as the theme it embraces. The opening stanza swings forth with the vigor and power appropriate to "poetic pains":

> What was he doing, the great god Pan,
>   Down in the reeds by the river?
> Spreading ruin and scattering ban,
> Splashing and paddling with hoofs of a goat,
> And breaking the golden lilies afloat
>   With the dragon-fly on the river.
>   (ll. 1—6)

In Pan's attempt to capture the nymph Syrinx, as Ovid tells us, Pan grabs a handful of reeds; for she has been metamorphosed by the river sisters in order to elude him. As he sighs through the reeds, they emit a plaintive, haunting melody which intrigues him. To the reeds he says, "you and I shall always talk together so!" [21] But Mrs. Browning departs from Ovid to have her great god Pan select a single reed, cut it short, draw the pith ("like the heart of a man" (l. 21), and notch it. Here, she has Pan say, is the only way to make sweet music. Then Pan deliberately blows through the pipe and makes piercingly sweet, sweet music—which revives the countryside and all of nature.

In a letter to Isa Blagden of April, 1860, Mrs. Browning refers to this poem as the last thing she had written and calls it "meek as a maid." [22] Apparently it was not so considered by everyone, for she mentions the poem again in a letter to Fanny Haworth, August, 1860, saying that one of her readers had written that the poem was "considered *immoral*";[23] but it is difficult for us to find any evidence of immorality in the poem. Half god, half beast, the great god Pan laughs by the river, "Making a poet out of a man" (l. 39), while the true gods sit up above and "sigh for the cost and pain,— / For the reed which grows nevermore again / As a reed with the reeds in the river" (ll. 40-42). Professor Taplin interprets the poem as having to do with the role of the poet as one of suffering and deprivation, for he is isolated from the satisfactions which ordinary men enjoy. [24] While there may be some suggestion of this theme in the poem, it is perhaps equally valid to read the poem as a statement about the Pan-poet who transforms nature through industry and imagination into art. Or perhaps it is better, after all, to read the poem as a delightful lyric suggested by the myth and leave it at that.

IX *"My Heart and I"*

In spite of the vigor of "Bianca Among the Nightingales," "A Musical Instrument," and some of the rousing propaganda of the political poems, Mrs. Browning is growing weary in her fifty-fifth year, and she knows she is in a state of declining health. In the very sensitive and beautiful lyric "My Heart and I," she describes the feeling:

> Enough! we're tired, my heart and I.
> We sit beside the headstone thus,
> And wish that name were carved for us.
> The moss reprints more tenderly
> The hard types of the mason's knife,
> As heaven's sweet life renews earth's life
> With which we're tired, my heart and I.
> (ll. 1–7)

The poem is clearly autobiographical in some respects but not in all. The speaker refers to Ralph, not to Robert; and it is Ralph who has said "Dear love, you're looking tired" (l. 26). But the enervation and lassitude of the last stanzas reflect what Mrs. Browning must have felt in this final year, when just walking on the balcony outside Casa Guidi, a thing she had done so much in the past, was too much for her. Typical also of her attitude is the dauntless last stanza, in which she expresses satisfaction that she has loved:

> Yet who complains? My heart and I?
> In this abundant earth no doubt
> Is little room for things worn out:
> Disdain them, break them, throw them by!
> And if before the days grew rough
> We *once* were loved, used,—well enough,
> I think, we've fared, my heart and I.
> (ll. 43—49)

Alethea Hayter has written of the last poems: "Some change in direction was beginning in Mrs. Browning's poetry which makes one long to know what she would have written if she had lived another ten years." [26] Miss Hayter wonders if Mrs. Browning, who was once "hot for certainties," may now have achieved that state, so admirably described by Keats, in which a man may move among uncertainties, mysteries, and doubts without any irritable reaching for solutions. [27] We can agree that in several of these last poems the poet speaks less spasmodically and with a purer lyricism than she does in any others, except in the *Sonnets from the Portuguese* and in one or two more of her other sonnets. It is quite possible that the quiet discipline of her final hours may well have subdued the "Pythian Shriek" (as Edmund Gosse termed it) [28] and fully freed the poetic voice. The wonderful "Bianca Among the Nightingales," the swingingly lyrical "A Musical Instrument," and the quietly effective "My Heart and I" make us wish Mrs. Browning had had those next ten years to write; but she did not. We must assess her in the light of what she has done, and while we may mourn for what might have been, we cannot judge her for it.

CHAPTER 8

Aurora Leigh: *The Artist as Woman*

P OSTERITY looks upon the *Sonnets from the Portuguese* and selected short lyrics as Elizabeth Barret Browning's major contribution to belles lettres. The poet herself, however, considered her verse-novels *Aurora Leigh* [1] to be her *magnum opus*. Published in 1856, the poem was in composition for at least eight years; but it was conceived in principle only some four years before the publication date. [2] In the letter to Browning, which confirms the actual date of conception, she announced her intention of writing a "novel-poem" in the same vein as "Lady Geraldine's Courtship." She saw the attempt as one which would destroy all of the old shibboleths once so dear to the heart of contemporary Victorians. In her dedication of the poem to John Kenyon, she wrote that *Aurora Leigh* contained within it her "highest convictions upon life and Art." [3]

Most scholars today know more about the critical commentary on the poem than they do about the work itself. Beginning with Edward FitzGerald's notorious statement recorded in his letter: "Elizabeth Barrett Browning is dead. Thank God, no more *Aurora Leighs!*" and ending with Samuel Chew's statement that Virginia Woolf "has said all that can be said, and more than most critics would say, for *Aurora Leigh,*" [4] we are left bemused but scarcely inspired to read the work itself. We are perhaps even less inspired to approach the work when confronted with the more than four hundred pages, ten thousand lines, and nine books of blank verse. Although the space limits of this study prohibit a very detailed treatment, we should consider it.

I *Narrative*

Aurora Leigh, heroine of the work, is the daughter of an Englishman and an Italian, fair-haired Florentine woman. After her mother's death in childbirth, Aurora and her father live in nature in Italy. The two strains of passion and learning reflected in her mother and her father, respectively, meet in Aurora Leigh, whose very name reflects the brilliant renaissance of culture of Italy and the intellectual toughness of England. At the age of four years, she enjoys the teachings of her father and the natural tutelage of nature. She lives among her father's books but is mesmerized by a portrait of her mother.

At the age of thirteen, she loses her father, who dies echoing in his final moment the word "Love." His death leaves the girl no choice but to return to England to live with a spinster aunt who has never quite forgiven Aurora's mother for marrying into the Leigh family. Aurora endures but never loves the frosty cliffs and cold fogs of England. While staying with her aunt and engaging in the rather meaningless tasks of sewing and embroidery, she meets her cousin Romney Leigh, a wealthy and philanthropically minded young man; he loves her; and she is not unattracted to him. His proposal, however, sends her to study and meditate in London; for he expresses himself in terms not calculated to endear himself to her poetic nature: he has asked her to marry him because, he says, he needs her to help with his various philanthropic ventures.

At age twenty, disinherited by her aunt, who dies, Aurora arrives in London—where she studies literature for seven long years. Here she is visited by the villainess of the piece, one Lady Waldemar, a cold, cruel woman who has designs on the rich and handsome Romney Leigh. Lady Waldemar tells Aurora that Romney, a man devoted to his various "good works," is about to marry a poor girl of the people, Marian Erle. Lady Waldemar, seeking to stop this marriage, has arrived in London to enlist Aurora's help. Aurora refuses to help, and Lady Waldemar storms out of her room.

Almost immediately thereafter, when Aurora seeks out Marian Erle, she finds her in a slum neighborhood where Marian relates the woeful tale of her childhood. She had been brutally treated by her parents while in the midst of the beautiful Malvern Hills; abandoned, she had wandered ill and alone until she ended in a ditch. Saved by a kindly waggoner and carried by him to a hospital, she had met Romney Leigh while he was making his rounds through the wards of the institution. He had secured for her a job with a seamstress, and in this position Marian has spent her time in thinking of the goodness of Romney and in helping her fellow workers in their hours of need. Romney, having rediscovered her in the midst of her good work, decides that the two should marry and consolidate their efforts in behalf of mankind. Aurora, hearing Marian's sweet story, agrees that such a marriage is desirable. At this point, Romney appears in the room and pronounces

the love of mankind far superior to "Romantic love." Aurora, hearing
this declaration, decides Romney is too coolly rational and abstract for
human understanding and leaves the couple with her blessing.

On the day of the Leigh-Erle wedding, Marian disappears. All of the
poor are there in rags and tatters, awaiting the celebration. When
Romney tells them that there will be no celebration, they become
obstreperous because of disappointment. Meanwhile, we are told that
Lady Waldemar has tricked Marian into thinking that Romney is
marrying her solely from his sense of obligation. Lady Waldemar has
induced Marian to leave with one of her friends, and she falls ultimately
into the hands of prostitutes and pimps. In Paris, the wicked city, she is
beaten, raped, and impregnated.

Romney knows nothing of this development, nor does Aurora. The
mob in attendance at the wedding riots out of disappointment and
attempts to kill Romney. Aurora faints upon seeing this violence. Later
on, Aurora receives a letter, sent by Marian to Romney, which
confesses that she is not worthy of Romney because she has fallen upon
evil times and has been led into evil ways. After this chaotic end of
events, Aurora and Romney part again, for he still believes that Art is a
frivolous toy compared with the profundities inherent in meeting the
needs of humanity. The first four books end here.

When Book Five opens two years later, Aurora is philosophizing
about art and poetry. She has heard that Romney has divided his
ancestral estate into almshouses and is continuing his good works and
also that Romney and Lady Waldemar plan to marry. Discouraged and
depressed by this news and, in addition, by an encounter at Lord
Howe's with Lady Waldemar, Aurora decides to seek haven and balm in
Italy. By these means she hopes not only to revive her spirits but also to
miss the wedding. When she arrives in Paris, en route to Italy, she sees
Marian Erle with a baby in her arms. She finally catches Marian, hears
her sad story, and takes Marian and the baby to Italy to live with her in
the midst of the beauty provided by nature. Part of Marian's story
involves the role played by Lady Waldemar in Marian's downfall.
Aurora is so sickened by the story that she wants to warn Romney, but
she hesitates to do so for fear of making him miserable in his marriage
to Lady Waldemar; for she believes, of course, that he has already
married this vicious creature.

Instead of writing to Romney, she writes to her friend Lord Howe to
tell him the full story of Marian's trials and sorrows; she then sends a
trenchant letter to Layd Waldemar, in which she denounces her for her

wicked conduct and warns her not to betray Romney Leigh; and finally she settles down to a quiet life with Marian and the baby. By a rough count, Aurora is now thirty and has been husbandless and somewhat lonely, but nonetheless still proud, for ten years. News of ' Romney filters through from England, but no one makes it clear to Aurora that he is now blind or that he has never married Lady Waldemar.

Book Eight opens with Romney's appearing on Aurora's terrace in Florence. Much talk ensues and much confusion results. He believes himself under obligation to Marian Erle, but she refuses to marry him because she wants to devote her life to her child alone. Aurora now knows that Romney is blind and unmarried. Finally, in Book Nine, they recognize their love for each other and agree to marry and work together out of love for the good of mankind.

II *Evaluation*

The plot has its counterpart in the melodramatic novels of the day. As Virginia Woolf has pointed out in *The Second Common Reader,*[5] the poem gives us what the plot does not—little Victorian vignettes, glimpses into drawing rooms, country gardens, churches, marketplaces. The skillful novelist would draw out the scene, turn it this way and that, rather than compress it as the poet has done. But *Aurora Leigh* is not a novel; it is a verse-novel, and, as such, it stands very much alone in the history of letters. Virginia Woolf has referred to it as a "masterpiece in embryo,"[6] because of its compression of thought and emotion where life and art are concerned with the high degree of contemporaneity the work reflects. For example, there are brilliant flashes of poetry in *Aurora Leigh,* but there is no steady flame. There is the philosophy of Aurora, which parallels that of Elizabeth: the poets should devote themselves to their own times and not to those long past. A strikingly effective passage underlines this point of view:

> Nay, if there's room for poets in this world
> A little overgrown (I think there is),
> Their sole work is to represent the age,
> Their age, not Charlemagne's,—this live, throbbing age,
> That brawls, cheats, maddens, calculates, aspires,
> And spends more passion, more heroic heat,
> Betwixt the mirrors of its drawing-rooms,

Than Roland with his knights at Roncesvalles.
To flinch from modern varnish, coat or flounce,
Cry out for togas and the picturesque,
Is fatal,—foolish too. King Arthur's self
Was commonplace to Lady Guenever;
And Camelot to minstrels seemed as flat
As Fleet Street to our poets.

(Bk. V, ll. 200—213)

This forthright accent on the asset of modernity as fit poetic mead places *Aurora Leigh* in the vanguard of the new thought. Furthermore, Mrs. Browning's recognition of the conflict between artist and woman adds a touch which makes that part of the work still valid for readers today. The reviews, however, affixed to the Porter-Clarke edition of the works, contain such diametically opposed critical opinions as to make the reader wonder if the reviewers could possibly be discussing the same work.

Blackwood's reviewer comments somewhat sneeringly on the poem and its author: "Mrs. Browning takes the field like Britomart or Joan of Arc, and declares that she will not accept courtesy or forbearance from critics on account of her sex." [8] The reviewer then proceeds to lambast the poem in terms more temperate but scarcely more laudatory than Margaret Fuller Ossoli's comment that Elizabeth had "the vision of a great poet, but little in proportion of his plastic power." [9] The poem was criticized, furthermore, for its exaggerated metaphors, the lack of verisimilitude in its characters, its similarity to Charlotte Brontë's *Jane Eyre*, its failure to portray the English classes as they really are, and, above all, for its coarseness and evidence of "unfeminine attitudes." [10]

On the other hand, J. Challen in the *National Quarterly Review* (1862) praises the poem highly, saying, "Aurora Leigh' is a great poem. It is a wonder of art. It will live." [11] And no less a member of the literati than Algernon Swinburne said: "No English contemporary poet by profession has left us work so full of living fire." [12] But the most elevated commentary of all comes from George Barnet Smith in "Poets and Novelists" when he says *Aurora Leigh* "is a poem which we could imagine Shakespeare dropping a tear over for its humanity . . . . To attempt to extract its beauty would be futile; it is a garden in which every flower of sweetness blooms. Its aroma is amongst the most fragrant in literature." [13]

Faced with such contrary points of view, the modern reader must and, in any case, should—exert his own judgment. *Aurora Leigh* was a "noble error"; the poet is to be commended for her effort, and for the sporadic but brilliant results that effort yielded. There is no question, however, that the total work is unwieldy, shapeless, amorphous, and philosophically untenable. While it will continue to be of interest to literary historians, it will never have much appeal for the general reading public (although an educated one) or, for that matter, for the mass of graduate students in English who seek a thesis topic with the urgent specter of "Time's winged chariot" behind them. For a work that reads so rapidly and reflects so readily the willingness of its Victorian author to strike out and immortalize the contemporary scene this fate seems unfortunate.

One additional comment might be made about the poem. The quality in *Aurora Leigh* that is reminiscent of Robert Browning's dramatic monologues. Whether this characteristic is owing to Elizabeth's use of ellipses or to her poetic eye's focusing and sketching detail much as a painter would is hard to say. A remarkable illustration of this exists in Book Three when Aurora is searching the slums for Marian Erle. And when the poet limns the scene in Saint Margaret's Court, where a sick child and a crude harlot (who stands in the window and curses her bed-ridden patient as well as Aurora) are portrayed with compassion through the eyes of Aurora Leigh:

> A sick child, from an ague-fit,
> Whose wasted right hand gambled 'gainst his left
> With an old brass button in a blot of sun,
> Jeered weakly at me as I passed across
> The uneven pavement; while a woman, roughed
> Upon the angular cheek-bones, kerchief torn,
> Thin dangling locks, and flat lascivious mouth,
> Cursed at a window both ways, in and out,
> By turns some bed-rid creature and myself.
> "Lie still there, mother! liker the dead dog
> You'll be to-morrow."
> (BK. II, 760-70)

Just such realistic passages brought down a Victorian storm of criticism about the head of Mrs. Browning, but such passages and others, not harsh but equally reflective of the world as it is, make the poem worth more from a literary point of view than critics have allowed: There are certain moments in *Aurora Leigh* when the poet equals her famous husband in ability to capture the quintessence of feeling. But the moments are rare, and the lack of continuity still makes this poem a "noble error."

CHAPTER 9

The Future Elizabeth Barrett Browning

V IRGINIA WOOLF wrote in 1932: "fate has not been kind to Mrs.
Browning as a writer. Nobody reads her, nobody discusses her,
nobody troubles to put her in her place. The primers dismiss her with
contumely. Her importance, they say, 'has become merely historical. . . .'
In short, the only place in the mansion of literature that is assigned her
is downstairs in the servants' quarters, where, in company with Mrs.
Hemans, Eliza Cook, Jean Ingelow, Alexander Smith, Edwin Arnold,
and Robert Montgomery, she bangs the crockery about and eats vast
handfuls of peas on the point of her knife." [1] In the current decade,
however, Mrs. Browning may well be moved from the kitchen and
reestablished in a proper room on the second floor of the "mansion of
literature." Professor Michael Timko suggested in 1968 that there is
great need for critical studies of her poetry as it relates her "life and
thought to her art," and he also states that there is urgent need for
sensitive studies of individual poems. [2]

Because of the need which Professor Timko has indicated, we have
tried in this study of Elizabeth Barrett Browning to present to the
reader an overview of her work which provides guidelines toward the
assessment of specific aspects of her contributions to belles lettres.
Reviewing those efforts, we see that the *Sonnets from the Portuguese*
still emerges, as critics in the past have stated, as her finest work. These
sonnets are the most ringingly lyrical of all her poems, but they are
somewhat more than just love lyrics. There is about them a kind of
tough-mindedness that many of her critics have overlooked. The
sonnets demand definitive treatment; for in them, more than anywhere
else in the canon, exists that profoundly intimate relationship among
life, thought, and art. Another area which has scarcely been entered is
that circumscribing the vast body of her letters. We have sampled them
and found them provocative, revealing, and delightful; but we have by
no means exhausted their resources. In conjunction with the sonnets,

the letters form the richest repository for Elizabeth Barrett Browning's thought and criticism. Moreover, her influence on Robert Browning and his on her still elude us, for the most part, but a careful study of her later works, notably *Casa Guidi Windows,* "Poems before Congress," and *Aurora Leigh,* with respect to the extent they reflect characteristics indigenous to the "dramatic monologue" (a genre perfected by Robert Browning), would surely prove illuminating.

As for a consideration of Elizabeth Barrett Browning as a poet, various themes and techniques emerge in her poetry; these, considered singly, indicate areas in which she appears more sharply original than former criticism suggests. For example, her use of baroque imagery and her interest in witchcraft and demonology might well prove more productive under intensive study than all the many comments extant concerning her interest in Spiritualism. Certainly, her knowledge of Plato and her reliance upon Platonic idealism would serve, if concentrated upon, to bring her religious themes into a wider and more accurate context. On the whole, the tension which grows from her reverence for the past and her commitment to the present have been inadequately treated. Far too often has she been relegated, if not to the kitchen, at best to the Victorian drawing room. The task for the future is obvious: she must be taken from both and given a room of her own (which for many years, we remember, she did indeed have), where she can once again speak with her authentic voice to informed listeners.

In this present study, we have seen Elizabeth Barrett Browning progress from the erudite, though imitative, juvenilia through the voluminous and chaotic efforts of the *Early Poems.* We have watched her struggle up Parnassus in the *Poems* of 1844 and achieve the heights evident in the *Sonnets from the Portuguese.* We have watched her emerge in the letters as woman, lover, comrade, artist. And, finally, we have watched her reach out to embrace those "men and women," who were Robert Browning's special forte, leaving her lyric voice a secondary note. Had she lived longer, she might have gone on to become more objective and intellectual in her poetry, as did Robert Browning himself in the many years that remained to him after her death. Certainly, in the later poems, she is reaching out farther for material, crossing cultural and class boundaries, and walking tall over issues and continents. But while she lived, we readily see a steady development from the spasmodic through the still clarion but controlled lyricism to the more intellectual and firmer final poems.

Additional and careful consideration of the corpus of her work should serve to establish her in her rightful place on the second floor of that mansion of literature where all major-minor Poets are deserving of a place. While Elizabeth Barrett Browning may never be seated on the first floor, she is still well on her way up out of the kitchen; and, for the discerning scholar and critic, her interest and her significance are far more than merely "historical."

Notes and References

Chapter One

1. I am deeply indebted in this chapter to Gardner Taplin's excellent critical biography, *The Life of Elizabeth Barrett Browning* (New Haven, 1957), which I used as a point of reference from which to verify facts found, though not always documented, in Dorothy Hewlett's highly readable biography, *Elizabeth Barrett Browning* (London, 1953). Very useful also was the definitive genealogical account by the late Jeanette Marks, *The Family of the Barrett* (New York, 1938), and Osbert Burdett's *The Brownings* (New York, 1936). Wherever desirable, I have consulted the letters of Elizabeth Barrett Browning to her husband, to her contemporaries, and to her family, with appropriate citation.

2. Hewlett, p. 10; Taplin, p. 10.

3. Quotations from the juvenile diary with the permission of John Murray Publishers and Miss Hannah French, Research Librarian, Wellesley College, Wellesley, Mass.

4. *Ibid.*

5. Taplin, p. 17; Hewlett, p. 30; see also Alethea Hayter, *Mrs. Browning: A Poet's Work and Its Setting* (London, 1962), Chapter 4, for a discussion of the effect of opium on her imagination and creativity, pp. 58–68; of. also note 28 *infra.*

6. *The Letters of Elizabeth Barrett Browning,* ed. Frederic G. Kenyon, 2 vols. (New York, 1910), I, 55–56; hereafter cited by short title, *Letters of EBB.*

7. Hayter, p. 14.

8. *Letters of EBB,* I, 242–43; see also I, 29–30, for an early allusion to Boyd's assistance in the reading of both Greek and Hebrew. See also *Elizabeth Barrett to Mr. Boyd,* ed. Barbara McCarthy (New Haven, 1955); hereafter cited as *Letters to Boyd.*

9. Burdett, p. 12; EBB was well aware of her limitations as a Greek scolar, as the following letter to Boyd affirms; *Letters to Boyd,* pp. 5–6.

10. Hewlett, pp. 34–35; in fact, "An Essay on Mind" was the poem

which prompted Hugh Boyd to seek out Elizabeth Barrett, according to the *Letters to Boyd,* p. xiv.

11. Taplin, p. 32; Hewlett, p. 43, gives the year as 1827.

12. See Marks, *The Family of the Barrett,* for an extensive treatment of this subject.

13. *Letters of EBB,* I, 19—20.

14. Hewlett, p. 53; Taplin, pp. 48—49.

15. Hewlett, pp. 52—54.

16. *Letters of EBB,* I, 43.

17. *Ibid.,* p. 47.

18. *Ibid., p 35.*

19. See Mrs. Sutherland Orr, *Life and Letters of Robert Browning* (New York, 1908), p. 131 (first published in 1891); see also Hayter, pp. 58—68. See also Elizabeth's letter of November 29, 1837, where she states that Dr. Chambers diagnosed her illness as "an excitability and irritability of chest." *Elizabeth Barrett to Miss Mitford,* ed. Betty Miller (New Haven, 1954), p. 22; hereafter cited as *Letters to Mitford.* The letters to Miss Mitford and to Mr. Boyd during this period are replete with references to "spitting blood" and to an "oppressive sense of weakness." Doctors Chambers and Barry are often mentioned by Elizabeth during this time.

20. On the years of Torquay, see Taplin, pp. 72—75, and Hewlett, p. 65.

21. Taplin, pp. 76—78; *Letters of EBB,* I, 73, 101, 102.

22. Hewlett, p. 70; Taplin, pp. 79—81.

23. *Letters of EBB,* II, 43—44.

24. *Ibid.;* note earlier letter to Mrs. Martin dated ca. August, 1851, pp. 14—15, and later letter to Miss Mitford, dated January 17, 1852; see also letter to Miss Mitford, pp. 44—45.

25. Taplin tells us that Elizabeth wrote "Queen Annelida and False Arcite" in the Chaucer edition. Her version followed the original closely, but the translation by Hunt and Bell did not (pp. 88—92). She began writing in 1839 to Horne, a popular author and critic, known for two tragedies *(Cosimo de Medici* and *Death of Marlowe),* a history of Napoleon, and the two works with which she was involved: *Chaucer Modernized* (1841), and *A New Spirit of An Age* (1844). See *Letters to Boyd,* p. 236, n. 4.

26. Taplin, pp. 84—85.

27. Hewlett, p. 75.

28. *Letters of EBB,* I, 134. Another revealing letter of this period (1842) was written to Miss Mitford about Elizabeth's need for opium in order to assuage her discomfort: "I say nothing against opium. It would be mere hypocrisy if I did. Under the denomination of morphine, I take life and heart and sleep and calm and am persuaded that it not only assuages the spirits but in my particular case it does positive *good* to the

lungs by equalizing the general circulation. Vivat opium! And may you and I leave its means!—moderation which is good in all things, say the copy books—being very particularly good, we must admit, in this." *Letters to Mitford*, pp. 155—56.

29. Hewlett, pp. 82—83; Taplin, pp. 108—10.

30. Taplin, pp. 117—18; see also Hayter, p. 17.

31. *The Letters of Robert Browning and Elizabeth Barrett*, ed. Robert Wiedeman Barrett Browning, 2 vols. (New York, 1899), I, 1—2; hereafter cited as *Love Letters*.

32. *Letters of EBB*, I, 236.

33. For a catalogue of the domestic problems concerning her relationship with her father, see the letter to Mrs. Martin (October 20, 1846), in which she refers to his "peculiar nature" and her "peculiar position" as deterrents to Robert Browning's making any formal proposal or request for her hand of Edward Moulton-Barrett *(Letters of EBB*, I, 286—97); see also letter to Mrs. Martin (September, 1851) for Elizabeth's reaction to the fact that her father had returned unopened all of those letters she had sent to him after her marriage to Robert Browning *(ibid.,* I, 20).

34. Hewlett, pp. 195—96.

35. *Letters of EBB*, I, 354—56.

36. *Ibid.,* II, 15.

37. *Letters of Robert Browning Collected by Thomas J. Wise,* ed. Thurman Hood (New Haven, 1933), p. 14.

38. *Letters of EBB*, I, 441

39. Letter from Rome, dated March, 1861, *ibid.,* II, 436.

40. For the story of her devotion to the ideal of Italian unification, see the discussion of her political poems in Chapter 7 in this study.

41. Her attitude toward England is strongly expressed at this time in a letter to John Kenyon written from Paris on July 7, 1851, *Letters of EBB*, II, 11—13; see also letter to Mrs. Jameson, *ibid.,* II, 23.

42. From a letter to Sarianna Browning, November 14, 1852, *Letters of EBB*, II, 94.

43. *Letters of Robert Browning Collected by Thomas J. Wise,* p. 62.

Chapter Two

1. Hewlett, p. 10.

2. Hayter (pp. 13—14) makes the point, however, that Elizabeth was dedicated to poetry as a vocation by the time she was eleven years old.

3. Taplin, p. 10.

4. *The Complete Works of Mrs. E. B. Browning,* ed. Charlotte Porter and Helen A. Clarke, 6 vols. (New York, 1901), I, 2. All quotations from Elizabeth Barrett Browning's poetry are from this edition, known as the Arno Edition, hereafter cited by short title, "Arno." Wherever

possible, citations to her poems appear in the text by volume and page or line numbers in parentheses.

5. Letter to Robert Browning, July 18, 1845, *Love Letters*, I, 129; in this same letter she admits that Coleridge's daughter was quite right to refer to the poem as a "girl's exercise."

Chapter Three

1. See Thomas Carlyle's *Sartor Resartus*, where man is conceived dualistically in the hero, Diogenes Teufelsdröckh), i.e., "God-born Devil's-dung."

2. Arno, I, 164–205.

3. See Chapter 7, Section VIII, in this study.

4. Hayter, pp. 35–36.

5. *Ibid.*, 34–36.

6. Irene Cooper Willis, *Elizabeth Barrett Browning* (London, 1928), p. 44.

7. Hayter, p. 30.

8. *Letters to Mitford*, pp. 38-39.

9. *Ibid.*, pp. 41–42.

10. *Ibid.*, *pp. 42–43.*

11. Willis, p. 33.

12. *Letters to Mitford*, pp. 155–56.

13. Hayter, p. 28.

14. *Ibid.*, pp. 27–30.

15. Arno, I, 114–16.

16. Arno, I, 272, note 53. "The Dream" is classified as "a fragment," but the poem appears to be finished—and effectively so. It is marred by those archaisms which Elizabeth was never to avoid entirely, regardless of the period in which she wrote. Such words as "wot," "sate," "erst," have little justification in a poem where we must assume the speaker to be a contemporary Victorian. Other than this defect, the poem stands as the best of this group. And there is no sound of weeping in it.

17. Arno, I, 104–5.

18. See Chapter 5, Section I in this study.

19. Arno, I, 116–17.

20. Arno, I, 273 *n.*

21. Arno, I, 112–13.

22. Arno, I, 272 *n.*

23. Hayter, pp. 82–83.

24. Before leaving these early poems on heroes, we might mention two poems addressed to the young Queen Victoria: "The Young Queen" and "Victoria's Tears" (Arno, II, 106–8, 108–10). Both speak of the young Queen's pious virtue, of her reliance upon God for

guidance, and of the tremendous tasks which lie ahead of her. Another poem concerned with the subject of youth worshiping a hero is "To Bettine" (Arno, II, 79–81), in which the young child-friend of Goethe, Bettina von Arnim, is lauded for her reverence of the great German poet. This bad poem is full of tears.

25. Arno, I, 118–21.
26. See Warner Barnes, *A Bibliography of Elizabeth Barrett Browning* (Austin, Texas, 1967), p. 73.
27. Elizabeth Barrett Browning, "A True Dream," *The Cornhill Magazine*, XXXVII (July, 1914), 21–24.
28. See discussion in Virginia L. Radley, *Samuel Taylor Coleridge*, Twayne's English Authors Series, No. 36 (New York, 1966), pp. 57–66.
29. Arno, I, 206–26.
30. See E. D. H. Johnson, *The Alien Vision of Victorian Poetry* (Hamden, Conn., 1963), pp. 10–11.
31. Arno, I, 168.
32. Harriet Waters Preston, ed., *Complete Poetical Works of Elizabeth Barrett Browning* (New York, 1900), pp. 14–20.
33. Arno, II, 1–10.
34. Hayter, p. 32.
35. Arno, II, 10–29.
36. Hayter, pp. 80–81.
37. *Letters to Boyd*, p. 255.
38. Hayter, p. 28.
39. Arno, II, 37–44.
40. Arno, II, 117–21.
41. Arno, II, 91–93. That Miss Barrett's enthusiasm for the sea knew no bounds is evident from "A Sea-side Walk" (Arno, II, 90–91), which, like "The Sea-Mew," is full of striking imagery. The mood of the sea, gray as the rocks with which it merges, is the "solemn beating-heart of nature," which is bound into man himself and is reflected in him by that mood which the memory of absent friends evokes, one of melancholy and sadness.
42. Hayter, p. 21.
43. Arno, II, 95–98.
44. See Chapter 5, Section I, in this study.
45. Arno, II, 44–48.
46. Arno, I, 151–52.
47. Arno, II, 29–37.

Chapter Four

1. *The Second Common Reader* (New York, 1932), p. 218.
2. Hayter, p. 79.

3. *Ibid.,* pp. 81—82.
4. Arno, II, 241—54.
5. In this letter To Hugh Boyd (1838), Miss Barrett states that the poem was written for Miss Mitford's *Finden's Tableaux,* but that it was too long for her own taste. *Letters of EBB,* I, 61.
6. Arno, II, 254—75.
7. Letter to Mr. Westwood, September 2, 1843, *Letters of EBB,* I, 150.
8. *Letters of EBB,* I, 61.
9. *Letters of EBB, I, 211.*
10. *Ibid.,* I, 177.
11. *Ibid.*
12. Ibid., I, 199.
13. *Love Letters, I, 32.*
14. *Letters of EBB,* I, 204.
15. Arno, II, 280—310.
16. See Arno, II, 381 *n.*
17. *Letters of EBB,* I, 181.
18. *Victorian Poets* (New York, 1897), pp. 130—31.
19. See *Early Victorian England,* ed. G. M. Young, 2 vols. (London, 1934), II, 426.
20. *Ibid.,* II, 87.
21. Arno, III, 53—59.
22. Letter to Hugh Boyd (1843), *Letters of EBB,* I, 153.
23. Arno, III, 134—40.
24. *Letters of EBB,* I, 179.
25. Arno, III, 147—58.
26. *Letters of EBB,* I, 128.
27. Arno, III, ix.
28. Arno, III, 97—106.
29. *Letters of EBB,* I, 247.
30. *Love Letters,* I, 10, 148, 270.
31. Letter to Hugh Boyd (1845), *Letters of EBB,* I, 247.
32. Arno, III, 1—29.
33. Hayter, pp. 80—86.
34. Stedman, pp. 124—26.
35. Arno, II, 149—226.
36. Taplin, p. 126.
37. *Ibid.,* p. 124.
38. Hayter, p. 75.
39. Arno, II, 144.
40. *Ibid.,* p. 145.
41. See Chapter 4, Section VI, in this study.
42. See Taplin, p. 126.

Chapter Five

1. Letter from Elizabeth to Robert Browning, September 12, 1846, *Love Letters*, II, 537.
2. *Letters to Boyd*, p. 94.
3. *Ibid.*, p. 24.
4. *Letters to Mitford*, p. 143.
5. Letters to Boyd, pp. 250–51.
6. Ibid., p. 254.
7. Ibid., pp. 254–55.
8. *Ibid.*, p. 257.
9. *Letters to Mitford*, p. 82.
10. *Ibid.*, p. 93.
11. *Ibid.*
12. *Ibid.*, p. 92.
13. *Ibid.*, p. 10.
14. *Ibid.*, p. xiii.
15. *Ibid.*, p. 81.
16. *Ibid., p. 78.*
17. *Ibid.*, pp. 178–79.
18. *Ibid.*, p. 172.
19. *Love Letters*, I, 8.
20. *Ibid.*, I, 6.
21. *Ibid.*, I, 22.
22. *Letters of EBB*, II, 370.
23. *Love Letters*, I, 24.
24. *Ibid.*
25. *Letters to Mitford*, p. 117.
26. *Ibid.*
27. *Ibid.*, p. 152.
28. *Love Letters*, I, 441.
29. *Letters to Mitford*, p. 116.
30. *Ibid.*
31. *Love Letters*, I, 25.
32. *Ibid.*, I, 448.
33. *Letters to Mitford*, p. 100.
34. *Love Letters*, I, 342.
35. *Letters to Mitford*, p. 82.
36. *Ibid., p. 145.*
37. *Ibid.*
38. *Ibid.*, p. 146.
39. *Ibid.*, p. 144.
40. *Ibid.*, p 145.
41. Ibid., p. 147.

42. *Ibid.*, p. 156.
43. *Letters of EBB*, II, 55–57.
44. *Love Letters*, I, 117.
45. *Letters to Mitford*, p. 141.
46. Betty Miller, *Robert Browning: A Portrait* (London, 1952), pp. 7–20 *et passim.*
47. *A Room of One's Own* (New York, 1929 and 1963).
48. *Letters to Mitford*, p. 9.
49. *Love Letters*, I, 8.
50. *Ibid., I, 129.*
51. *Ibid.*, I, 129–30.
52. Letter of January 4, 1840, *Letters of the Brownings to George Barrett*, ed. Paul Landis (Urbana, Ill., 1958), p. 43; hereafter cited by short title, *Letters to George Barrett.*
53. *Ibid.*, p. 114.
54. *Ibid.*, p. 142. See also *Love Letters*, II, 314–23, letters dated July 7, 8, 9, and 10.
55. Letter dated Friday, July 10, 1846, *Letters to George Barrett*, p. 144.
56. Letter of September 17–18, 1846, *ibid.*, p. 148.
57. *Ibid.*, p. 152.
58. See letters of September 6, 1860, and April 2, 1861, *Letters to George Barrett*, pp. 235–40, 255–57.
59. *Ibid.*, Introduction, pp. 1–34.
60. *Love Letters*, I, Note, p. v.
61. *Ibid.*, I, 481.
62. *Ibid.*,I, 1.
63. *Ibid.*, I, 3.
64. *Ibid.*, I, 4.
65. *Ibid.*, I, 11.
66. *Ibid.*, I, 12.
67. *Ibid.*, I, 203.
68. *Ibid.*, I, 405.
69. *Ibid.*
70. *Letters to George Barrett*, p. 14.
71. Letter of September 18, 1845, *Love Letters*, I, 211.
72. Letter of September 25, 1845, *ibid.*, I, 222.
73. *Ibid.*, I, 223.
74. Letter of September 16, 1845, *ibid.*, I, 203.
75. See letters of April 8 and 9, *ibid.*, II, 46–52, 52–54.
76. Letter of April 9, *ibid.*, II, 55.
77. In the summer of 1966, I saw Marylebone Church with its Browning chapel. While the church was damaged during World War II, it is still a stately and solid edifice.

78. *Love Letters*, II, 538.
79. Friday night, September 19, 1846, *Love Letters*, II, 562.

Chapter 6

1. *Love Letters*, II, 351—52.
2. *Ibid.*, II, 353.
3. Elizabeth Barrett Browning, *Sonnets from the Portuguese*, ed. Fannie Ratchford, *Variorum Edition* (New York, 1950), pp. 26—34; hereafter cited by short title *Variorum*.
4. *Variorum*, p. 27.
5. Edmund Gosse, "Sonnets from the Portuguese," in *Critical Kit-Kats*, Vol. III (London, 1913; first published 1897); see also Gosse, "Origin of the 'Sonnets from the Portuguese,' " *Critic*, XXV (December 8, 1894), 398. For evidence to the contrary, see John Carter and Graham Pollard, *An Enquiry into the Nature of Certain Nineteenth-Century Pamphlets* (New York, 1934).
6. *Variorum*, pp. 29—30.
7. Hayter, p. 105 *et passim*.
8. *Ibid.*
9. *Ibid.*
10. *Ibid.*
11. *Variorum*, p. 37; all quotations from the *Sonnets* are from this edition, and wherever possible, citations will appear within the text, in parentheses, by page number.
12. Hayter, p. 108.
13. *Love Letters*, 42—43.
14. *Ibid.*, I, 67.
15. *Ibid.*, I, 44.
16. See *Love Letters*, I, 209, where Mr. Barrett will not sanction her proposed trip to Pisa.
17. Heilman, *The Explicator*, IV (October 14, 1945), Item 3.
18. Going, *The Explicator*, XI (June 11, 1953), Item 58.
19. Plato, *Symposium*, trans. Benjamin Jowett.
20. *Love Letters*, I, 500.
21. *Ibid.*, I, 501.
22. *Ibid.*, I, 503; see also letter of August 17, 1846, in which EBB writes: "and surely I have loved you, in the idea of you, my whole life long." *Love Letters*, II, 431.
23. *Letters to Mitford*, p. 273.
24. *Ibid.*
25. *Ibid.*, p. 275.
26. Letters to Mitford, p. 275; see also *ibid.*, pp. 264—65.
27. *Ibid.*, p. 274.

28. *Love Letters,* I, 351.

29. *Ibid.,* I, 350—51.

30. See Chapter 8.

31. For a solid and clear explanation of the sonnet forms, see Paul Fussell, Jr., *Poetic Meter and Poetic Form* (New York, 1965), Chapter 6.

32. Hayter, p. 107.

33. *Ibid.,* p. 106.

34. *Love Letters,* I, 45—46.

Chapter Seven

1. Arno, III, 249, her own statement on the genesis of the poem.

2. Arno, III, 250—13.

3. Arno, III, xv.

4. Hayter, pp. 120—21.

5. *Ibid.,* p. 124.

6. Arno, III, 316—58.

7. Arno, III, 315.

8. See Gordon Craig, *Europe Since 1815* (New York, 1961), pp. 185—90.

9. See Trevelyan, pp. 512—13.

10. Arno, II, 46—47.

11. Arno, II, 48—50.

12. Arno, II, 59—61.

13. Arno, II, 71—76.

14. Arno, II, 39—44.

. Arno, II, 9—14.

16. Arno, VI, 14—20.

17. Arno, VI, 34—39.

18. Hayter, pp. 223—24.

19. Arno, VI, 20—21.

20. Arno, VI, 44—45.

21. See *Metamorphoses,* trans. Rolfe Humphries (Bloomington, Ind., 1955), Book I, pp. 24—25.

22. *Letters of EBB,* II, 377.

23. *Ibid.,* II, 406.

24. Taplin, p. 388.

25. Arno, VI, 31—33.

26. Hayter, p. 225.

27. *Ibid.,* pp. 225—26.

28. See *ibid.,* p. 194.

Chapter Eight

1. Arno, IV, 2–158, Books I–IV; V, 1–196, Books V–IX.
2. See letter to Robert Browning, February 27, 1845, which attests to this letter. *Love Letters*, I, 321.
3. Arno, IV, 11.
4. *A Literary History of England*, ed. Albert C. Baugh (New York, 1948), p. 1403.
5. Woolf, *The Second Common Reader* (New York, 1932), pp. 218–31.
6. *Ibid.*, p. 225.
7. See appendixes to Arno, Vols. IV and V.
8. Arno, IV, 215.
9. Arno, V, 247.
10. Arno, IV, 230, an excerpt from the *Edinburgh Review*, 1861.
11. Arno, IV, 233.
12. Arno, V, 258.
13. Arno, V, 254.

Chapter Nine

1. Virginia Woolf, The Common Reader: Second Series (New York, 1932), p. 219.
2. Michael Timko, "Elizabeth Barrett Browning: A Review of the Year's Research," *The Browning Newsletter*, I (October, 1968), 3–6.

Selected Bibliography

PRIMARY SOURCES

1. *Works*

Aurora Leigh. New York: C. S. Francis and Co., 1857. Note from Elizabeth on flyleaf states that she received sufficient remuneration from Mr. C. S. Francis to insure him of sole rights to her poem, *Aurora Leigh.*

Elizabeth Barrett Browning's Poetical Works. New York: Dodd, Mead and Co., 1885.

Poems, from The Last London Edition. New York: Worthington, 1889.

Complete Poetical Works: ed. Harriet Waters Preston. Boston and New York: Houghton Mifflin, 1900. Probably the most available edition to today's reading public; omits many poems and most of the prose.

The Complete Works of Elizabeth Barrett Browning. Ed. with Introduction and Notes by Charlotte Porter and Helen A. Clarke. New York: Thomas Y. Crowell and Co., 1900. 6 vols. Known as the Coxhoe Edition, this edition follows the author's latest revision, which appeared in a six-volume edition under the supervision of Robert Browning. Contains the notes and difficult-to-obtain prose work.

The Complete Works of Mrs. E. B. Browning. Ed. Charlotte Porter and Helen A. Clarke. New York: George D. Sproul, 1901. 6 vols. This edition was brought out in a package with an additional twelve volumes of the poetry of Robert Browning. Only 1250 copies were printed; and the edition, known as the Arno, is based on the Coxhoe. Notes and references are the same as those in the 1900 Coxhoe. The Arno edition, however, is in larger type, more manageable, and contains a photograph of the Story sculpture of Elizabeth Barrett Browning. This is the standard edition used in this study.

"A True Dream," *The Cornhill Magazine,* XXXVII (July, 1914), 21–24.

Elizabeth Barrett Browning: Hitherto Unpublished Poems and Stories with an Inedited Autobiography.. Edited by H. Buxton Forman. Boston: The Bibliophile Society, 1914. 2 vols. Limited edition of 453 copies printed for members of the Bibliophile Society. Contains an early autobiography of Elizabeth written when she was fourteen, at Hope End. The MS now rests in the Wellesley College Library. Appendix includes notes of Elizabeth's written while on her trip to Paris in 1815. Interesting juvenilia includes poems to mother, father, brother, and sisters.

Casa Guidi Windows. Florence: Giulio Giannini and Sons, 1926.

Sonnets from the Portuguese. Centennial Variorum Edition. Ed. Fannie Ratchford, with Notes by Deoch Fulton. Duschnes, 1950. Text of the sonnets based on the 1856 edition, authorized and corrected by poet herself. Traces the evolution of the sonnets through the three manuscripts: Morgan Library (M), the British Museum (B), and the Houghton Library (H).

2. *Letters*

Letters of Elizabeth Barrett Browning Addressed to Richard Hengist Horne. Ed. S. R. Townshend Mayer. London, Richard Bentley and Son, 1877. 2 vols.

The Letters of Robert Browning and Elizabeth Barrett, 1845–1846. Ed. Robert Wiedemann Barrett-Browning. New York and London: Harper and Brothers, 1899. 2 vols.

The Letters of Elizabeth Barrett Browning. Ed. with biographical additions by Frederic C. Kenyon. First published in 1897. New York: Macmillan, 1910. 2 vols. in 1. Good cross-section of her letters, but much of the biographical information is now superseded. Contains letters to Boyd, Horne, Mitford, Jameson, Martin, Blagden, Chorley, John Kenyon, Sarianna Browning, Miss Haworth *et al.*, on a variety of subjects. Of particular interest are letters concerning contemporary literature.

Letters to Robert Browning and Other Correspondents by Elizabeth Barrett Browning. Ed. Thomas J. Wise. London: n.p., 1916. Printed for private circulation; only one letter was written by the poet.

Elizabeth Barrett Browning: Letters to Her Sister, 1846–1859. Ed. Leonard Huxley. London: John Murray, 1931. These letters to Henrietta Barrett did not come to light until seventy years after the publication of the Kenyon letters in 1897. Contains 107 letters with supplementary letter or postscript from Robert Browning. Chiefly of interest for biographical minutiae.

Twenty-two Unpublished Letters of Elizabeth Barrett Browning and Robert Browning addressed to Henrietta and Arabella Moulton-Barrett. New York: The United Features Syndicate, 1935.

Contains the correspondence which remained unpublished after Leonard Huxley had selected letters for his 1929 edition. Also contains an interesting note by J. A. S. Altham, grandson of Captain Surtees Cook, husband of Henrietta Moulton-Barrett.

Letters From Elizabeth Barrett to B. R. Haydon (1842–45). Ed. Martha Hale Shackford. New York: Oxford University Press, 1939. Contains eighteen autograph letters and three fragments from the Palmer Collection at Wellesley College.

Elizabeth Barrett to Miss Mitford: Unpublished Letters . . . . Ed. Betty Miller. New Haven: Yale University Press, 1954. Contains literary anecdotes, bits of critical commentary, opinions on a variety of subjects from dogs to social and political reform. Contains 142 of the total 381 unpublished letters (1836–46) in the Wellesley College library.

Elizabeth Barrett to Mr. Boyd: Unpublished Letters . . . . Ed. Barbara P. McCarthy. New Haven: Yale University Press (for Wellesley College), 1955. Letters reflect admiration for Boyd; contain indications of the poet's early literary enthusiasms and working habits.

Letters of the Brownings to George Barrett. Ed. Paul Landis. Urbana, Ill.: University of Illinois Press, 1958. Interesting collection because poet's letters to George differ markedly from those to sisters. Her opinions on literary figures of the age, on past and present poetry and prose are here recorded. Appendix contains letters from her physicians; notes identify people who came within her orbit.

3. Miscellaneous Primary Sources

BROWNING, ROBERT. *Letters of Robert Browning Collected by Thomas J. Wise.* Ed. Thurman L. Hood. New Haven: Yale University Press, 1933. Collected by Wise after the Browning sale of 1913, when the papers of both poets were widely scattered. Letters give fine portrait of Browning before and after the fifteen years with Elizabeth.

————. *New Letters of Robert Browning.* Ed. William Clyde De Vane and Kenneth Leslie Knickerbocker. New Haven: Yale University Press, 1950. 2 vols. Short letters from Browning. About one quarter of Vol. I contains letters written while Elizabeth was still living. Of interest is letter to Sarianna and Robert Browning, Sr., June 19, 1861, written a few hours after her death.

————. *Browning to His American Friends.* Ed. Gertrude Reese Hudson. New York: Barnes and Noble, 1965. Letters from 1841 to 1890. Includes letters from Robert Browning and Elizabeth to the Storys and James Russell Lowell. Also includes their replies. In addition, a collection of the correspondence between Robert

W. Barrett-Browning and his parents' friends (with their replies).
Interesting for the light shed posthumously on both parents.

MCALEER, EDWARD C. Learned Lady: Letters from Robert
Browning to Mrs. Thomas Fitzgerald. Cambridge, Mass.: Harvard
University Press, 1966. Includes sixty-six letters from the Carl H.
Pforzheimer Library which, in the main, had hitherto been
unpublished. Interesting for insights into the personality of
Robert Browning and his son after the death of Elizabeth.

SECONDARY SOURCES

ADLER, ADRIENNE. "Elizabeth Barrett Browning, Christina Rossetti,
Dante Gabriel Rossetti, and George Meredith: Love Sonnet
Sequence in Victorian Poetry." Unpublished master's thesis,
Duke University, 1964. Treatment of the *Sonnets from the
Portuguese* rests heavily upon the sensation, emotion, and
thought evoked in Elizabeth by her love for Robert Browning.

ALEXANDER, DOROTHY. "Elizabeth Barrett Browning, An Expression of Her Time." master's thesis, Columbia University,
1928. Emphasizes importance of the social and historical background of the period in which she wrote.

BAKER, HARRY T., "Mrs. Browning's Sonnets," *Saturday Review of
Literature,* V (April 13, 1929), 895. In a letter to the Editor, Mr.
Baker takes exception to Louis Untermeyer's comments
("Colossal Substance," *ibid.,* March 16, 1929) concerning the
"obscurity" of the *Sonnets from the Portuguese.*

BENSON, ARTHUR CHRISTOPHER. *Essays.* N.p., 1896. Laudatory
commentary on the poet in which Benson sees her as speaking a
"universal language" (213).

BOAZ, LOUISE S. *Elizabeth Barrett Browning.* New York: Longmans,
Green and Co., 1930. Popular rather than scholarly biography: no
documentation, no bibliography. Not useful to the scholar but
readable for an overview of her life. Most interpretations are
accurate; little out-and-out lionizing.

BOOTHBY, EDITH MORTIMER. "The Influence of Personal and
Social Environment upon the Poetry of Elizabeth Barrett
Browning." Boston: Unpublished Thesis, Library, Boston
University, 1931. Attempts to demonstrate the impact that social
and historical conditions in England and Italy had upon her
choice of theme and subject matter. Some emphasis upon
Christian allusions and use of natural imagery.

BRADFIELD, THOMAS. "The Ethical Impulses of Mrs. Browning's
Poetry," *Westminster Review,* CXLVI (August, 1896), 175–84.
Suggests that she herself was impelled to write such poems out of

her own ethical attitude; also discusses style and form in her poetry.

BURDETT, OSBERT. *The Brownings.* New York: Houghton Mifflin, 1936. The lives of both Brownings, compressed into one volume, the primary contribution of Burdett's highly readable book. Some factual errors exist, but serves as a quick introduction to the Brownings' lives and their poetry.

BUTLER, FRANCIS H., "Sonnets from the Portuguese," *Academy,* LXVI (March 5, 1904), 258. Letter in reply to a question asked regarding the source of the word "crystalline" in Sonnet XV.

CARTER, JOHN, and GRAHAM POLLARD. *An Enquiry into the Nature of Certain Nineteenth Century Pamphlets.* New York: Charles Scribner's Sons, 1934. Fascinating account of the method by which these two men exposed the "Reading" edition of the *Sonnets from the Portuguese.*

COLLINS, THOMAS J. *Robert Browning's Moral-Aesthetic Theory: 1833–1855.* Lincoln: University of Nebraska Press, 1967. Of significance are pages 127–36 where, in a section treating "of love," Dr. Collins examines the influence of Elizabeth Barrett Browning on Browning's concept of love.

CRESTON, DORMER. *Andromeda in Wimpole Street.* New York: E. P. Dutton and Co., 1930. Interesting account of the romance of Elizabeth Barrett and Robert Browning which takes her from age seven at Herefordshire to her death in Italy and burial in Florence. A popular account but the author draws on Elizabeth's letters and includes an account of Hope End, its environs, and 50 Wimpole Street.

CROWELL, NORTON B. *The Triple Soul: Browning's Theory of Knowledge.* Albuquerque: University of New Mexico Press, 1963. Attempts to refute the view of Browning as an anti-intellectual and a "Romantic" by demonstrating the importance of mind as one of the facets necessary to Browning's world view. The others are "body" and "spirit." The concluding chapter mentions Elizabeth's importance in the shaping of the "triple soul" (p. 226); remarks also that her letters are better and more "closely reasoned" than Browning's (226).

CUNNINGTON, S., "Sonnets from the Portuguese," *Academy,* LXVI (February 13, 1904), 181. Answer to inquiry concerning the meaning of a few lines in Sonnet XV; sees parallels in her selection of diction with that of Shakespeare and some other Elizabethans.

DICK, E., "Sonnets from the Portuguese," *Academy,* LXVI (February 6, 1904), 157. When Gosse stated that there were no forced rhymes in the *Sonnets* he left himself open to the kind of criticism reflected in Dick's letter.

DODDS, M. H., "Sonnets from the Portuguese," *Notes and Queries* (November 2, 1946), 193. Concerned with Sonnet XVIII; discusses the significance of the word "plant" in terms of whether it should have had a substitution the word "plait."

FIELD, KATE, "Elizabeth Barrett Browning," *Atlantic Monthly* (September, 1861), 368–76. Eulogizes the poet, her appearance, conversation, decorative taste highly laudatory commentary on her poetry. Typical of much of the criticism of the late nineteenth century concerning Elizabeth Barrett Browning.

FUSSELL, PAUL. *Poetic Meter and Poetic Form.* New York: Random House, 1965. Helpful handbook to understanding the forms of poetry. Discussion of elements of a good Petrarchan sonnet (pp. 124–28) used in this study as basis of comparison with *Sonnets from the Portuguese.*

GAY, ROBERT, "Elizabeth Barrett Browning's *Sonnets from the Portuguese,*" *The Explicator,* I (December, 1942), Item 24. Discussion of the imagery, "fire-tipped wings" of "two souls" in Sonnet XXII, as connotative of the cherubim on the Ark of the Convenant who faces each other reflecting spiritual love.

GAYLORD, HARRIET, "Gosse and the 'Reading Sonnets,'" *Times Literary Supplement,* November 8, 1934, p. 775. Letter in which Miss Gaylord produces a letter from Lilian Whiting stating that Browning first saw the MS of the *Sonnets from the Portuguese* in Bagni di Lucca in 1849, not in 1847.

————. "The Human Side of EBB," *Saturday Review of Literature,* XII (August 24, 1935), 9. Letter to the Editor makes the point that her humor, wit, whim, and teasing tone are reflected in many of her works and thus form an important aspect of her character.

GILDER, RICHARD WATSON, "The Romance of the Nineteenth Century: Robert Browning and Elizabeth Barrett," *Century,* LXX (October, 1905), 918–27. Sees her in the Italian tradition of the sonnet. Believes Sonnet XIII nearest to perfection.

GOING, WILLIAM, "Elizabeth Barrett Browning's *Sonnets from the Portuguese,*" *The Explicator,* XI (June 11, 1953), Item 58. Refutes Robert Heilman's objection to the famous Sonnet XLIII, "How do I love thee?" and finds it abstractions justifiable.

GOLDSTEIN, MELVIN. "Elizabeth Barrett Browning's 'Sonnets from the Portuguese' in the Light of the Petrarchan Tradition." Ph.D. dissertation, University of Wisconsin, 1958. Thorough study of her sonnet sequence in the light of the tradition; She kept the orthodox rhyme scheme upon which her contemporaries insisted but permitted herself a fuller use of language in which Classical and contemporary allusion interweave in order to amalgamate intellect and emotion. This dissertation should be made available to all through publication.

GOSSE, EDMUND, "Sonnets From the Portuguese." *Critical Kit-Kats.*
Vol. III. London: William Heinemann, 1913. Began the hassle
over whether or not there was an 1847 edition of the *Sonnets;*
tells a pretty story of how Elizabeth presented the sonnets to
Robert Browning: unfortunately, the story is false.

————. "Origin of the 'Sonnets from the Portuguese,' " *Critic,* XXV
(December 8, 1894), 398. Another of the numerous articles
concerning the publication date of the *Sonnets.*

GREEN, DAVID, "E. Barrett to Hugh Stuart Boyd: An Additional
Letter," *Publications of the Modern Language Association,*
LXXVI (March, 1961), 154—55. Discusses a letter from Elizabeth
to H. S. Boyd, the blind Classics scolar, in which she comments
upon her religious opinions: she was never "orthodox" in her
beliefs. Because she is often presented as a saccharine Christian,
this commentary provides a needed antidote.

HAGEDORN, RALPH, "Edmund Gosse and the 'Sonnets from the
Portuguese,' " *Bibliographical Society Papers,* XLVI, 67—70.
States that Gosse insisted on the 1847 date of publication of the
Sonnets even though he knew of Lilian Whiting's statement in her
book that the two poets' son had said that the *Sonnets* were
unknown to his father until three years after the marriage.

HAYTER, ALETHEA. *Mrs. Browning: A Poet's Work and Its Setting.*
London: Faber and Faber, 1962. Excellent discussion of her
experiments with rhyme and meter. More critical than descriptive
of poem but most recent critical study.

HEILMAN, ROBERT B., "Elizabeth Barrett Browning's 'Sonnets From
the Portuguese,' " *The Explicator,* IV (October 14, 1945), Item
3. Criticizes Sonnet XLIII; says it is as embarrassing as all
platform rhetoric with its abstract imagery and glaring generalizations which have no relation to concrete experience.

HEWLITT, DOROTHY. *Elizabeth Barrett Browning.* London: Cassell
and Co., 1953. One of two most recent biographies of EBB (the
other is Gardner Taplin's). Miss Hewlett's was to be the standard
biography of the poet while Mr. Taplin's was to be the "critical"
biography. Miss Hewlett's book is informative and lively but
sparsely documented. Good on her personality.

HOPKINS, ANNETTE B., "Poet Laureate of Hope End," *South
Atlantic Quarterly,* XXX (July, 1931), 290—308. Discusses the
early autobiographical "diary" MS in Wellesley College library.

INGRAM, JOHN H. *Elizabeth Barrett Browning.* Boston: Roberts
Brothers, 1888. Initial full-length biography; written before
letters available to the public. Superseded by more recent
biographies but interesting for the early critical estimate of the
poet before her reputation declined.

LEWIS, NAOMI, "The Genius of Elizabeth Barrett Browning," *Listener* (July 20, 1961), 91–92. Touches upon the *Sonnets, Aurora Leigh*, and "Lady Geraldine's Courtship"; stresses personality rather than craftsmanship.

LOTH, DAVID. *The Brownings, A Victorian Idyll.* New York: Tudor Publishing Co., 1935. "Fictionalized" biography contains many errors; of no use to the serious student of either of the Brownings.

LUBBOCK, PERCY. *Elizabeth Barrett Browning is Her Letters.* London: Smith, Elder and Co., 1906. Based on her letters; helpful to the general reader; of little use to the serious student and scholar because the citations and references are inadequate.

MARKS, JEANNETTE. *The Family of the Barrett.* New York: The Macmillan Co., 1938. Contains much useful information on the backgrounds of both the Moulton-Barretts and the Brownings; explores common West Indian heritage from private collection, files of letters from Jamaica, Barbados, Bermuda, etc. Little if any literary criticism but explores social and cultural climates which produced *Aurora Leigh*. Indispensable to Barrett-Browning scholars.

MARSON, CLOTILDA, "The 'Reading' Sonnets," *Times Literary Supplement* (November 15, 1934), 795. Supports the argument that Browning did not see the *Sonnets from the Portuguese* until 1849.

MILLER, BETTY. *Robert Browning: A Portrait.* London: John Murray, 1952. Psychological-literary study of Robert Browning as mother dominated; his romance with Elizabeth as a search for a mother substitute—one who remained idealized and firmly set on a pedestal. Supports point of view solidly.

MORGAN, EDWIN, "Women and Poetry," *Cambridge Journal,* III (August, 1950), 643–73. Elizabeth Barrett Browning is not a successful poet because she is a woman. The author makes this interesting statement: "The urge to create is rare in women because it is an irritation and an aspiring and indeed an anguish, which the ordinary tenor of their lives need never admit." However, Elizabeth did not enjoy an "ordinary tenor."

MOULTON, CHARLES WILLS, ed. *The Library of Literary Criticism.* Vol. VI. New York: Peter Smith, 1935. Compendium of critical commentary on the *Sonnets from the Portuguese;* includes statements by William T. Arnold, James Ashcroft Noble, R. H. Stoddard, Anne T. Ritchie, William Sharp, Eugene Schuyler, A. E. Cross, Margaret Oliphant, and Arthur Benson. Helpful to those wishing a quick introduction to the criticism before 1935.

ORR, MRS. SUTHERLAND. *Life and Letters of Robert Browning.* Revised and rewritten in part by Frederic G. Kenyon. New York: Houghton Mifflin, 1908. First published in 1891 by personal friend of the poets'. After the publication of the *Love Letters* and Kenyon's edition of her letters, much of Mrs. Orr's book became obsolete; for this reason Kenyon rewrote sections.

PEATTIE, ELIA W., "Love and Death," *Harper's Bazaar,* XLV (September, 1911), 408—09. *Sonnets from the Portuguese* faulty in technique and effect; does not present an adequate case. Marred by effusiveness over the Browning romance.

PHILLIPSON, JOHN, "How Do I Love Thee—An Echo of St. Paul," *Victorian Newsletters,* XXII (Fall, 1962), 22. Holds that she, in using imagery similar to Paul, elevates the temporal to the eternal and thereby gives the temporal a sacred character.

SMITH, FRED MANNING, "Mrs. Browning's Rhymes," *PMLA,* LIV (September 1939), 829—34. Compares her experiments in rhyme to those of Archibald MacLeish, W. H. Auden, C. Day-Lewis; supports the contention that her rhyme "defects" were intentional with excerpts from her letters; suggests influence upon Emily Dickinson.

SMITH, GROVER, "Petronius Arbiter and Elizabeth Barrett," *Notes and Queries* (November 2, 1946), 190. Shows that certain elegiac verses of Petronius Arbiter resemble her first sonnet in the *Sonnets from the Portuguese.*

STEDMAN, EDMUND CLARENCE. *Victorian Poets.* New York: Houghton Mifflin and Co., 1897. First published in 1875; a good example of criticism which lauded Elizabeth Barrett Browning over Robert Browning. Stedman, however, repeatedly makes the point that she is the best "female poet" since Sappho—thereby qualifying his critical estimate of her poetic talents.

STODDARD, RICHARD HENRY, "The Sonnet in English Poetry," *Scribner's Monthly,* XXII (1881), 905—21. Discusses mainly the history of the sonnet form through Sidney, Spenser, Daniel, Shakespeare, Donne, Milton, Herbert, Wordsworth, and Keats, but also refers to Mrs. Browning's earliest sonnets written in the Petrarchan tradition. Stoddard finds them technically good but believes them harsh, strained, and artificial. *Sonnets from the Portuguese* good; reveal her personal expression of her love for another.

TAPLIN, GARDNER, "Mrs. Browning's Poems of 1850," *Boston Public Library Quarterly* (October, 1957), 181—94. Discusses the emendations made in the sonnets before publication in the edition of 1849—50. Contains a clear explanation of the title of her sequence, *Sonnets from the Portuguese.*

————. "Mrs. Browning's Contributions to Periodicals: Addenda," *Papers of the Bibliographical Society of America,* 44 (1950), 275—76.

————. *The Life of Elizabeth Barrett Browning.* New Haven: Yale University Press, 1958. Excellent bibliography, includes editions, contributions to periodicals, collections and descriptions thereof, publications of her letters, pp. 455-66. The biography itself is the most recent; dubunks the love story somewhat.

THACKERAY AND HIS DAUGHTER, ed. Anne Thackeray Ritchie. New York: Harper and Brothers, 1924. Interesting comments on Elizabeth, Robert Browning by the novelist's daughter.

THOMPSON, FRED C., "Elizabeth Barrett Browning on Spiritualism: A New Letter," *Victorian Newsletter,* No. 31 (Spring, 1967), 49–52 Letter to John Westland Marston, December 14, 1853, shows her attempting to temper her unshakable faith in Spiritualism with a rational approach.

TIMKO, MICHAEL, "Elizabeth Barrett Browning: A Review of the Year's Research," *The Browning Newsletter,* I (October, 1968), 3–6. Important for citing directions scholars might wish to take in investigating her work.

THORPE, JAMES, "Elizabeth Barrett's Commentary on Shelley," *MLN,* LXVI (November 1951), 455–58. Reproduction of commentary in margins of collection of Shelley's works. One of favorite poets; first introduction to prose. Objected only to religious ideas and inaccuracy in Greek translation.

TOD, ALEXANDERA CHARLOTTE. "Elizabeth Barrett Browning as a Lyric Poet." Unpublished doctoral dissertation. The University of Manitoba, 1927. Holds that she was a lyric poet of emotional sincerity. Her greatest themes, love and religion, were those which culminated in poetry of high lyric quality. Chapter 5 discusses her contention that poetic art exists for the purpose of showing human will in cooperation with Divine Will. The relationship between God and each Human Soul provides mankind with the highest object for contemplation.

WARD, MAISIE. *Robert Browning and His World: The Private Face, 1812–1861.* New York: Holt, Rinehart and Winston, 1967. Chapter 7, devoted to Elizabeth Barrett, discusses the extent to which her father and opium influenced her early adult years. The rest of the book contains almost as much information on her as it does on Robert Browning and ends with her death. Some insights and information exist here that are either buried or slighted in other studies.

WAUGH, ARTHUR. *Reticence in Literature.* London: Westminster Press, 1915. In a discussion of the poetry of emotion and mood, the author points to the vitality and sympathy which Victorian poetry received as a result of her influence. While aware of the faults in her poetry, praises the *Sonnets from the Portuguese* as poems "inspired by great passion for life." Interesting for assessing the tenor of criticism in the early part of this century.

WHITING, LILIAN. *A Study of Elizabeth Barrett Browning.* Boston: Little, Brown and Co., 1902. First published in 1899, this study suffers from inaccuracies. Miss Whiting's book on both Brownings *(Their Life and Art)* is superior to this study.

————. *The Brownings, Their Life and Art.* Brown and Co., 1911. Detailed study of the daily lives of the Brownings; not very helpful on the poetry. Inscribed to Robert Barrett Browning (Pen) with whom Miss Whiting spent hours in conversation. Contains certain information (chiefly minutiae) not readily available elsewhere.

WILLIS, IRENE COOPER. *Elizabeth Barrett Browning.* London: Gerald Howe, Ltd., 1928. Small volume from the series entitled "Representative Women." More an appreciation of the poet than a critical biography; no documentation and no bibliography.

[WINWAR, FRANCES] GREBANIER, FRANCES. *Immortal Lovers: Elizabeth Barrett and Robert Browning.* New York: Harper and Brothers, 1950. Highly romanticized accounts of the Brownings, their love affair, subsequent marriage. More substantial in presentation of facts than the Loth monograph, but of little use to scholars. Probably the most enjoyable, best written of the popular biographies.

WISE, THOMAS J., "Mrs. Browning's Sonnets, 1847," *Times Literary Supplement* (May 24, 1934), 380. Claims that the Reading Edition of 1847, although not intended for circulation, was the first privately printed edition and not a forgery. Wise, for whatever his reasons, was wrong.

WOOLF, VIRGINIA. *The Second Common Reader.* New York: Harcourt, Brace, 1932. Commentary on *Aurora Leigh* still merits consideration.

————. *A Room of One's Own.* New York: Harcourt, Brace, 1929 and 1963. Discussions of the woman as artist help to shed light on Elizabeth's problem of one hundred years before.

BIBLIOGRAPHIES

BARNES, WARNER. *A Bibliography of Elizabeth Barrett Browning.* The University of Texas and Baylor University, 1967. The only descriptive bibliography of Elizabeth Barrett Browning's work since the Wise bibliography; reliable bibliography is essential to students of the poets for it points out the Wise forgeries and urges caution. Made use of the Hinman Collating Machine and contains substantive textual variants which will be useful to future scholars. Lists 500 books not included in Wise. Broken down into English and American, with descriptions of Wise forgeries.

COOKE, JOHN D., AND LIONEL STEVENSON. *English Literature of the Victorian Period.* New York: Appleton-Century-Crofts, 1949. Very brief account of the poet's life coupled with a minimal listing of her major works and a few critical articles.

EHRSAM, THEODORE G., ROBERT DEILY, AND ROBERT SMITH. *Bibliographies of Twelve Victorian Authors.* New York: The H. W. Wilson Company, 1936. To 1936, the most complete bibliograpy; contains full-length studies and significant periodical articles.

FAVERTY, FREDERIC E., ed. *The Victorian Poets: A Guide to Research.* Cambridge, Mass.: Harvard University Press, 1956. Useful as a general reference for background of the Victorian period. Bibliographical essay by A. McKinley Terhune (pp. 84–92) covering bibliography, biography, works, letters, and criticism.

SLACK, ROBERT C. *Bibliographies of Studies in Victorian Literature for 1955–1964.* Chicago: University of Illinois Press, 1967.

TEMPLEMAN, WILLIAM. *Bibliographies of Studies in Victorian Literature for Thirteen Years, 1932–1944.* Chicago: University of Illinois Press, 1945.

Victorian Bibliography, 1932–1958. May issue of *Modern Philology.*

Victorian Bibliography, 1958 to Present. June issue of *Victorian Studies.*

Wellesley Index to Victorian Periodicals 1824–1900.

WISE, THOMAS J. *Bibliography of the Writings in Prose and Verse of Elizabeth Barrett Browning.* Privately printed, 1918. Wise's notoriety as a bibliographer is now well known; superseded by Warner Barnes.

WRIGHT, AUSTIN. *Bibliographies of Studies in Victorian Literature for Ten Years, 1945–1954.* Chicago: University of Illinois Press, 1956.

Index

(The works of Elizabeth Barrett Browning are listed under her name)